Introductory Financial Accounting

Using International Financial Reporting Standards

2nd Edition

by

John McCallig

DONMORRIS BOOKS
Dublin

This edition published 2008 by DONMORRIS BOOKS.
The first edition published 2007 by DONMORRIS BOOKS.

ISBN 978-0-9561329-0-1

DONMORRIS BOOKS
PO Box 11513, Blackrock, Co. Dublin, Ireland.

Printed in Ireland by Naas Printing

Contents

Chapter 1

A Guided Tour of a Set of Financial Statements

Introduction

Each year thousands of business entities all over the world spend countless hours and resources preparing financial statements and distributing them to their owners and other parties. These financial statements contain financial information about the performance and resources of the business and are used by a wide variety of users. Figure 1.1 gives a list of possible users developed by the International Accounting Standards Board [IASB].

Figure 1.1
Extract from IASB Framework for the Preparation and Presentation of Financial Statements [1]

The users of financial statements include present and potential investors, employees, lenders, suppliers and other trade creditors, customers, governments and their agencies and the public. They use financial statements in order to satisfy some of their different needs for information. These needs include the following:

(a) *Investors.* The providers of risk capital and their advisers are concerned with the risk inherent in, and return provided by, their investments. They need information to help them determine whether they should buy, hold or sell. Shareholders are also interested in information which enables them to assess the ability of the entity to pay dividends.

(b) *Employees.* Employees and their representative groups are interested in information about the stability and profitability of their employers. They are also interested in information which enables them to assess the ability of the entity to provide remuneration, retirement benefits and employment opportunities.

(c) *Lenders.* Lenders are interested in information that enables them to determine whether their loans, and the interest attaching to them, will be paid when due.

---

[1] IASC, 1989, "International Financial Reporting Standards - Framework for the Preparation and Presentation of Financial Statements" Para. 9

Figure 1.1
Extract from IASB Framework for the Preparation and Presentation of Financial Statements [2] (continued)

(d) *Suppliers and other trade creditors.* Suppliers and other creditors are interested in information that enables them to determine whether amounts owing to them will be paid when due. Trade creditors are likely to be interested in an entity over a shorter period than lenders unless they are dependent upon the continuation of the entity as a major customer.

(e) *Customers.* Customers have an interest in information about the continuance of an entity, especially when they have a long-term involvement with, or are dependent on, the entity.

(f) *Governments and their agencies.* Governments and their agencies are interested in the allocation of resources and, therefore, the activities of entities. They also require information in order to regulate the activities of entities, determine taxation policies and as the basis for national income and similar statistics.

(g) *Public.* Entities affect members of the public in a variety of ways. For example, entities may make a substantial contribution to the local economy in many ways including the number of people they employ and their patronage of local suppliers. Financial statements may assist the public by providing information about the trends and recent developments in the prosperity of the entity and the range of its activities.

The IASB state that "the objective of financial statements is to provide information about the financial position, performance and changes in financial position of an entity that is useful to a wide range of users in making economic decisions." The IASB therefore regard usefulness in decision making as the primary function of financial statements. While this may seem un-contentious, in fact it was once though that the primary function of financial statements was the protection of people or organizations that were owed money by the business entity. In some countries, until recently, the primary function of financial statements was to calculate the tax liability.

Financial statements are prepared under the national laws of the state in which the company is situated and the accounting rules of that jurisdiction. In the European Union financial statements of companies listed on stock exchanges must now be prepared under International Accounting Standards [IAS]. These standards provide guidelines on how particular accounting numbers should be calculated. They also specify information that should be disclosed in the

[2] IASC, 1989, "International Financial Reporting Standards - Framework for the Preparation and Presentation of Financial Statements" Para. 9

financial statements. In most countries, the legal framework for financial statements is quite broad. For example in the UK and Ireland legislation requires the annual preparation of financial statements and their approval at the Annual General Meeting of a company [AGM]. Legislation also requires that financial statements give a 'True and Fair View.' However, all the detailed rules as to how numbers in the financial statements are calculated are taken from Accounting Standards.

Financial statements consist of three main reports. The statement of financial position reports on the resources owned by the business entity and the amounts owed by the entity. The income statement reports on how much profit has been generated by the business entity. The statement of cash flows reports on the amount of cash that has been received and paid out of the business.

The Statement of Financial Position[3]

The statement of financial position shows the assets, liabilities and equity of the business entity. Figure 1.2 shows the IASB definitions of these terms.

Figure 1.2
Extract from IASB Framework for the Preparation and Presentation of Financial Statements [4]

The elements directly related to the measurement of financial position are assets, liabilities and equity. These are defined as follows:

(a) An ***asset*** is a resource controlled by the entity as a result of past events and from which future economic benefits are expected to flow to the entity.
(b) A ***liability*** is a present obligation of the entity arising from past events, the settlement of which is expected to result in an outflow from the entity of resources embodying economic benefits.
(c) ***Equity*** is the residual interest in the assets of the entity after deducting all its liabilities.

An asset could be a building, a vehicle, an item of stock, a bank balance or an amount due from a customer. The key point in the definition above is that the resource is 'controlled' by the entity. For example, leased assets are not legally

[3] The statement of financial position was previously known as the balance sheet.

[4] IASC, 1989, "International Financial Reporting Standards - Framework for the Preparation and Presentation of Financial Statements" Para. 9

owned[5] by a business but they are often 'controlled' by the entity and treated as if they were owned. In this case, IAS rules demand that the leased asset is treated in the same way as an asset that is legally owned by the entity. The second part of the definition states that future economic benefits are expected to flow from an asset. For example, if an entity purchases a building it can expect accommodation benefits to flow from that building for a long time. If the entity shows receivables[6] as an asset they are assuming that cash will flow from these customers over time.

Liabilities are amounts that are owed by the entity to a third party. They could be amounts owed to suppliers, to banks or to the government.

Equity is the amount by which assets exceed liabilities. To understand this concept, consider buying a house for €500,000 and getting a loan of €400,000 to finance this purchase. You own the house so your asset is worth €500,000. You owe €400,000 to the bank so this is a liability. The difference between your assets and your liabilities is €100,000 and this is your equity stake in the house. In the same way, company shareholders are the residual claimants for company assets. This means that they get whatever assets are not claimed by others. Suppose that a company's assets were €1m and its liabilities were €600,000. If the company were shut down and all the assets were sold and all the liabilities were paid off there would be €400,000 left in the company that could be paid out to the shareholders.

It is important to appreciate that the statement of financial position is prepared at a point in time. It is like a photograph in that it shows a 'freeze frame' of what things were like at a particular moment. It is also like discussing your bank balance. It is only meaningful to say 'I had €400 in the bank at 4pm today.' If you don't specify a time and date you might have had that money in the bank 25 years ago which is not very useful information. Have look at Table 1.1 which show the Group Statement of Financial Position for CRH plc, an Irish building supplies company. Notice that the title states 'as at 31st December 2007.' This is the date at which the statement of financial position is calculated.

The figures in the statement of financial position are recorded mainly at 'historic cost.' This means that the assets are recorded at their original cost. For example, a building purchased 25 years ago for €2,000 might still be shown at

---

[5] Leasing involves purchasing the services of an asset by making lease payments over a period of time. Legally the asset remains the property of the lease company during the period of the lease. Often, after the last lease payment is made the asset is transferred to the entity that used the asset.
[6] Receivables are amounts due from customers. They were previously called 'Debtors' under UK Accounting rules.

this amount[7]. Many different valuation bases could be used in the financial statements. These include the replacement cost of the asset, the current selling price or the value to the business. Each of these valuation bases is used in special circumstances but historic cost is the main valuation base that is used. It has the advantage of being easy to verify for an auditor, although it my not be the most relevant value for an asset.

When we think of the value of a firm like Microsoft it is obvious that the value of that firm depends on the future cash flows that can be generated from its market position and its intellectual capital. Accountants find such measures very difficult to define and explain so, for the most part, they are ignored. Accountants only recognize an asset where they can see a probable economic benefit in the future and where there is a cost or value that can be measured with reliability[8]. For example, if Microsoft buys an office chair then this is a cost that can be measured reliably and presumably the chair will have economic benefits in the future in that an employee can sit down and be more productive. The transaction of purchasing the chair will give rise to changes in financial records and be recorded in the financial statements. On the other hand, suppose Microsoft had just signed a contract to supply a very large new customer with software for 5 years into the future. We can argue that this has economic benefits in the future, but they are very hard to measure so accountants would typically ignore this event until Microsoft actually started to ship goods as part of the new contract. This means that resources like intellectual capital, staff knowledge and experience, brand value and technology are omitted from the statement of financial position.

This deliberate understatement of the statement of financial position is called 'conservatism.' The effect of conservatism is to delay the recording of profits or gains until they are reasonably certain and to accelerate the recording of losses. For example, if it becomes apparent that an asset is worth more than its value on the statement of financial position then accountants wait until the asset is actually sold to recognize that value. In contrast to this, if it becomes apparent that an asset is worth less than its statement of financial position value then this fall in value must be immediately recorded in the financial statements.

The 'Going Concern' principle means that statement of financial position is usually prepared using the assumption that the firm will continue in operation for the foreseeable future. Figure 1.3 gives the definition from the IASB.

---

[7] Or even less if the asset had been depreciated.

[8] IASC, 1989, "International Financial Reporting Standards - Framework for the Preparation and Presentation of Financial Statements" Para. 83

Figure 1.3
Extract from IASB Framework for the Preparation and Presentation of Financial Statements[9]

The financial statements are normally prepared on the assumption that an entity is a going concern and will continue in operation for the foreseeable future. Hence, it is assumed that the entity has neither the intention nor the need to liquidate or curtail materially the scale of its operations; if such an intention or need exists, the financial statements may have to be prepared on a different basis and, if so, the basis used is disclosed.

For example, buildings are usually shown on the statement of financial position at their original cost less depreciation. Depreciation is the accountant's measurement of how much of the benefits from the building have been used up. This is fine if we can assume that the business will continue and that it will be able to use the benefits from that building. If the company is in financial trouble and it is likely the building may have to be sold then it may make more sense to value the building at its 'open market' or 'sale' value rather than at original cost less depreciation.

It is necessary to look at one more concept before we look at the statement of financial position. That is the concept of 'Group' or 'Consolidated' financial statements. Most large companies are not organized as one legal company unit. Instead they have a holding company that holds some or all of the shares in a number of other companies. Modern multinational enterprises require complex group structures for many reasons. Group companies may be required in order to minimize taxation and to operate in different regulatory environments. In the distant past companies were allowed to report only the financial statements of the holding company. The financial statements for this legal unit are almost completely meaningless. This concept lives on under UK GAAP in that companies still report a statement of financial position for 'the company' and a consolidated statement of financial position for the group. Accounting rules started to insist that companies report their financial statements for the economic entity rather than the legal entity. The process of combining the financial statements for a number of related companies is called consolidation. In common with other areas of accountancy it is difficult to develop a set of rules that capture the economic significance of the relationships between companies in all possible situations. Accounting rules define three different types of Group Company. A brief explanation of each follows:

[9] IASC, 1989, "International Financial Reporting Standards - Framework for the Preparation and Presentation of Financial Statements" Para. 23

Subsidiaries

A subsidiary company is controlled by the main company and must be fully consolidated into the main companies' financial statements. This consolidation process means that the financial statements of the group of companies are prepared 'as if' all of the group companies were one economic entity. Readers of financial statements prepared in this way can have some assurance that all of the group's assets and liabilities have been included in the consolidated financial statements.

Associates

Associate companies are companies in which the main company holds a substantial holding but does not fully control. These companies are accounted for using what is called the 'equity' method of accounting. This means that the main company brings in its share of the associate's income into its income statement. However, assets and liabilities of the associates do not appear on the main company's statement of financial position.

Investments

If the main company has only a small holding in another company then these holdings are carried at cost as financial investments in the Statement of financial position. If the value of these investments falls below cost then their value in the statement of financial position should be reduced.

Now that we have discussed the basic principles used to construct the statement of financial position have a look at Table 1.1 which contains the statement of financial position of CRH plc. CRH plc, headquartered in Ireland, has operations in 24 countries, employing approximately 60,000 people at over 2,100 locations. Their operations focus on primary building materials, value-added building products and specialist building materials distribution. Table 1.1 shows figures for the statement of financial position 'as at' 31st December, 2007 and 31st December, 2006.

Table 1.1 CRH Group Statement of Financial Position as at 31st December[10]

Notes		2007 €m	2006 €m
	ASSETS		
	Non-current assets		
13	Property, plant and equipment	8,226	7,480
14	Intangible assets	3,692	2,966
15	Investments in associates	574	554
15	Other financial assets	78	97
23	Derivative financial instruments	124	74
26	Deferred income tax assets	336	489
	Total non-current assets	13,030	11,660
	Current assets		
17	Inventories	2,226	2,036
18	Trade and other receivables	3,199	3,172
23	Derivative financial instruments	9	5
21	Liquid investments	318	370
21	Cash and cash equivalents	1,006	1,102
	Total current assets	6,758	6,685
	Total assets	19,788	18,345
	EQUITY		
	Capital and reserves attributable to the Company's equity holders		
29	Equity share capital	186	184
29	Preference share capital	1	1
30	Share premium account	2,420	2,318
30	Own shares	(19)	(14)
30	Other reserves	70	52
30	Foreign currency translation reserve	(547)	(137)
30	Retained income	5,843	4,659
		7,954	7,063
31	Minority interest	66	41
	Total equity	8,020	7,104

[10] CRH plc's full financial statements are available on http://www.crh.ie

Table 1.1 CRH Group Statement of Financial Position as at 31st December[11] (continued)

	LIABILITIES		
	Non-current liabilities		
22	Interest-bearing loans and borrowings	5,928	5,313
23	Derivative financial instruments	52	47
26	Deferred income tax liabilities	1,312	1,301
19	Trade and other payables	141	160
27	Retirement benefit obligations	95	262
25	Provisions for liabilities	248	320
28	Capital grants	11	10
	Total non-current liabilities	7,787	7,413
	Current liabilities		
19	Trade and other payables	2,956	2,788
	Current income tax liabilities	244	216
22	Interest-bearing loans and borrowings	570	645
23	Derivative financial instruments	70	38
25	Provisions for liabilities	141	141
	Total current liabilities	3,981	3,828
	Total liabilities	11,768	11,241
	Total equity and liabilities	19,788	18,345

The first section in the statement of financial position deals with '**Non-current Assets.**' These are assets that are used on a continuing basis in the business. There are three main classes of non-current assets in the statement of financial position. Property, plant and equipment have a physical presence. In the case of CRH plc, they consist of factories, buildings, vehicles, mines, machines and all other fixtures and fittings. Intangible assets are non-current assets that do not have a physical presence. The main item within this section is 'Goodwill.' Goodwill arises when one company acquires another. If the amount paid for the company's shares exceeds the fair value of the assets acquired then goodwill will be created. Financial assets consist of any investments CRH has made in other companies. For example, if CRH plc acquired 10% of the shares in another company then the cost of this investment would be regarded as a financial asset.

The second section in the statement of financial position deals with '**Current Assets.**' These are assets that are expected to be short-term in nature. In other words, we expect the economic benefits from these assets to be received in the

[11] CRH plc's full financial statements are available on http://www.crh.ie

next year. Typically, current assets contain amounts for inventories, receivables and cash. The cash balance is simply the amount of money the organization has in the bank[12]. Inventory is the amount of raw materials, work-in-progress and finished goods that the company has at the end of the reporting period. Inventory is valued at 'the lower of cost and net realizable value.' This means that stock is usually valued at what it cost to make or to buy but if the amount it will be sold for goes below cost we must use the lower amount. Receivables[13] are the amount owed to the group by its customers. The amount owed by customers should be reviewed each year for 'bad debts.' These are individual customers who may not be willing or able to pay their debts.

Current assets are more 'liquid' that non-current assets. This means that the economic value associated with these items can be converted into a liquid asset such as cash more quickly than non-current assets. Obviously, the cash balances are the most liquid assets. The receivables are the next most liquid asset as they should be received in about 3 to 6 months. Inventory is the least liquid current asset as it would probably take a long time to organise a 'fire sale' of the stock. Selling the inventory quickly would probably involve giving customers large discounts which would reduce the amount that could be liquidated quickly.

Moving to the bottom of the statement of financial position, **Current liabilities** include any bank overdrafts, creditors and taxes due. Trade payables[14] are amounts due to the firm's suppliers. They will have to be paid in about the next 3-4 months. The amount for tax is the amount of tax that is due on our profits but has not yet been paid over to the Government. Long-term liabilities are called **'Non-current liabilities'** in IFRS financial statements. The main item here is usually loans from financial institutions. These loans differ from current liabilities in that they will have to be repaid over a long period of time like 10 years.

The **'Equity'** section of the statement of financial position shows the residual interest in the assets of the entity after deducting all its liabilities. This can be represented by the accounting equation.

---

[12] Cash is a confusing term. Accountants usually refer to demand deposit accounts in the bank as 'cash.'

[13] Also known as 'Debtors.'

[14] Payables are also known as 'Creditors.'.

Figure 1.4
The Accounting Equation

Assets – Liabilities = Equity

Or

Assets = Equity + Liabilities

This equation states that equity is the residual or surplus of assets less liabilities. This surplus belongs to the owners of the business entity. For example, consider a business with assets of €1,000 and liabilities of €700. The equity in this business in €300 (€1,000-€700) and is owed back to the owners of the business. If the business were shut down then the liabilities of €700 could be paid off leaving €300 for the owners of the business. In a limited company the owners of the business are the shareholders. When the company was set up a certain number of shares will have been issued. Further shares can be issued as the business needs more capital. These shares will have been paid for by the shareholders and the amount they contributed for the shares is divided into two parts. Firstly, equity share capital is the number of shares issued multiplied by the 'par' or 'nominal' value of the shares. The 'par' or 'nominal' value is the unit price of the shares which is set when the company is created. It is often €1. The second part of equity share capital is the share premium. This is any excess over the par value of the shares that shareholders have been willing to pay. For example, suppose a company was set up with a par value of the shares of €1.00 each. The founder of the company then buys 100 shares for €1.00 each. This gives the company share capital of €100.00. One year later, the company needs more share capital and it issues another 50 shares. This time the shares are sold at €1.20. The share capital would now be 150 shares at €1.00 each plus **'Share Premium'** of €10.00 (50 shares x €0.20 each.)

Table 1.2

	Before any shares issued	**Issue of 100 shares**	**Issue of 50 extra shares**
	€	**€**	**€**
Issued share capital	0	100	150
Shares of €1.00 each			
Share premium	0	0	10
	0	100	160

The issued share capital plus the share premium represents the amount of money that has been contributed by the shareholders. The rest of the firm's equity will have been generated internally rather than contributed by the shareholders. Consider a firm that starts off with equity of 100 shares by €1.00 each. The owner(s) of the shares will have contributed €100 in cash which will have been lodged to the firm's bank account. This €100 is used to buy goods that the firm subsequently sells for €130. At the end of this transaction the firm has assets of €130 as compared to assets of €100 at the start of the transaction. The €30 extra is the firm's profit. If you look at the accounting equation, assets have increased and liabilities have not changed so equity must change to keep the equation in balance.

Table 1.3

	Before the transaction	**Purchase and sale**	**Issue of 50 shares**
	€	**€**	**€**
Assets	100	-100+130	130
- Liabilities	0	-	0
	100		130
Issued share capital	100	-	100
Shares of €1.00 each			
Retained profit	0	+30	30
	100	-	130

The Income Statement

This point brings us to the **Income Statement**. This is the second of the main financial reports and was called 'The Profit and Loss Account' under UK/Irish GAAP. The income statement shows how much profit has been generated by the firm during the year. As was discussed above we could do this by looking at how much the net assets (assets less liabilities) had grown during the year. The income statement uses an alternative approach. Instead of looking at how much assets and liabilities changes it looks at income and expenditure.

Figure 1.4
Extract from IASB Framework for the Preparation and Presentation of Financial Statements [15]

The elements of income and expenses are defined as follows:

(a) Income is increases in economic benefits during the accounting period in the form of inflows or enhancements of assets or decreases of liabilities that result in increases in equity, other than those relating to contributions from equity participants.

(b) Expenses are decreases in economic benefits during the accounting period in the form of outflows or depletions of assets or incurrence of liabilities that result in decreases in equity, other than those relating to distributions to equity participants.

The income statement accumulates items over a time period rather than providing a snapshot at a particular point in time. For example, the income statement given in Table 1.3 shows income and expenses 'for the year ended 31 December 2007.' The revenue or sales figure in this income statement is composed of all of the sales transactions that CRH plc made during this period. The measurement of the items in the income statement is governed by the accruals principle. The IASB definition of the accruals principle is given in Figure 1.5 below:

Figure 1.5
Extract from IASB Framework for the Preparation and Presentation of Financial Statements [16]

In order to meet their objectives, financial statements are prepared on the accrual basis of accounting. Under this basis, the effects of transactions and other events are recognised when they *occur* (and not as cash or its equivalent is received or paid) and they are recorded in the accounting records and reported in the financial statements of the periods to which they relate. (emphasis added)

The accruals principle says that transactions should be recorded in the financial statements when they occur rather than when they are received or paid in cash. Take a sales transaction for example. Sales are usually on credit so the main events in a sale are the sales order, the delivery of the goods and the payment for the goods. The accruals principle says we should record the sale in our financial statements when it occurs (usually when the goods are delivered)

[15] IASC, 1989, "International Financial Reporting Standards - Framework for the Preparation and Presentation of Financial Statements" Para. 70

[16] IASC, 1989, "International Financial Reporting Standards - Framework for the Preparation and Presentation of Financial Statements" Para. 22

rather than wait until we are paid for the goods. So when we look at the income statement all the income and expenses included are those that occurred during the period rather than those received or paid in cash during the period.

Take a look at the CRH plc, Group Income Statement given in Table 1.4

Table 1.4 CRH plc Group Income Statement[17] for the financial year ended 31st December

Note		2007 €m	2006 €m
1	**Revenue**	20,992	18,737
	Cost of sales	(14,715)	(13,123)
	Gross profit	6,277	5,614
3	Operating costs	(4,191)	(3,847)
1,4,5	**Group operating profit**	2,086	1,767
1	Profit on disposal of fixed assets	57	40
1	Profit before finance costs	2,143	1,807
8	Finance costs	(473)	(407)
8	Finance revenue	170	155
9	Group share of associates' profit after tax	64	47
	Profit before tax	1,904	1,602
10	Income tax expense	(466)	(378)
	Group profit for the financial year	1,438	1,224
	Profit attributable to:		
	Equity holders of the company	1,430	1,210
31	Minority interest	8	14
	Group profit for the financial year	1,438	1,224
12	**Basic earnings per Ordinary Share**	262.7c	224.3c
12	**Diluted earnings per Ordinary Share**	260.4c	222.4c

The first figures in the income statement give the groups **'Revenue'** and **'Cost of Sales.'** Revenue is the total of all sales that occurred during the accounting period. Cost of sales is the cost of either making or buying in the goods or

[17] CRH plc's full financial statements are available on http://www.crh.ie

services that were sold during the period. Cost of sales includes what we call 'production' costs. It would include the cost of materials, production labour and factory overheads like depreciation on machinery. It does not include any expenses that relate to management, administration, marketing or distribution. All of these costs are included in **'Operating Costs.'** The next major line in the income statement is 'Group Operating profit.' This figure is the amount of profit generated from the firm's operations. Interest and taxation are then deducted from profits and after some other adjustments the **'Group Profit for the Financial Year'** is arrived at. This figure is the amount of profit that could be added to the equity of the firm in this year.

Summary

The statement of financial position and the income statement are the two primary components of a firm's financial statements. The statement of financial position shows the assets, liabilities and equity of a firm at a particular point in time. The income statement shows how the firm's equity has changed over time. The income statement calculates the change in equity by summing the firm's income and subtracting the firm's total expenses.

Chapter 1 Exercises

Exercise 1.1

Have a look at the full financial statements of CRH Group plc for the year ended 31/12/2007. Note the types of information that is given in the financial statements. The full report is available at www.crh.ie

Exercise 1.2

Classify each of the following items as an asset, a liability or equity:

Buildings
A bank loan
Cash in the bank
Payables
Tax due to the government
Receivables
Inventory
Share capital
Retained income

Exercise 1.3

Which of the following items would meet the definition of an asset of ABC plc? Provide an explanation of your answer in each case.

- Land owned by ABC plc.
- A car owned by Jane Murphy who is a director of ABC plc.
- Rent owed to ABC plc by DEF plc.
- €1,000 which will be owed to ABC plc by TRF plc when ABC plc delivers goods to TRF plc.
- €10,000 which has been spent on researching a new product that ABC plc will manufacture
- €50,000 which has been spent on repairing the roof of ABC plc's warehouse.

Exercise 1.4

For each of the following 6 companies, one or more figures are missing. The missing figure can be calculated using the accounting equation of:

Assets = Liabilities + Equity

	Assets	Liabilities	Equity
1	295	117	?
2	11,961	?	3,215
3	?	1,911	2,816
4	106,412	62,372	?
5	?	9,383	?
6	19,495	12,713	?

Exercise 1.5

The following information relates to three separate companies. In companies B and C some figures are missing.

	A plc	B plc	C plc
Share capital of €1 each	3,000	5,000	?
Plant and machinery	2,000	1,000	6,000
Cash/Bank	100	200	Nil
Loan payable (2020)	2,000	1,000	Nil
Inventory	400	2,000	3,500
Land and buildings	2,500	6,000	2,000
Receivables	1,300	3,000	1,500
Payables	300	1,000	2,000
Bank overdraft	700	Nil	1,500
Retained income	1,200	?	4,000
Loan receivable (short term)	900	Nil	2,000

Requirement:

You are required to reconstruct the statement of financial position for each of the companies, using the attached formats, clearly indicating the missing figures.

Statement of financial position

	A plc	B plc	C plc
Non-current assets:			
Land and buildings			
Plant and machinery			
Total non-current assets			
Current assets:			
Inventory/Stock			
Receivables (Debtors)			
Loan receivable			
Cash/Bank			
Total current assets			
Total assets			
Equity			
Share capital of €1 each			
Retained			
Total equity			
Non-current liabilities			
Long term loans			
Current liabilities:			
Payables (Creditors)			
Bank overdraft			
Total liabilities			
Total equity and liabilities	7,200	12,200	15,000

Exercise 1.6

The following data relate to **Cosmos Ltd** at 31 March 20X1 based on its first trading year ended on that date.

	€
Payables	60,000
Closing inventory	40,000
Receivables	90,000
Plant and Machinery	185,000
Land at cost	105,000
Buildings	110,000
Equity share capital	250,000
Retained income	65,000

Note: Some figures required for the balance are missing. However, you may assume that total current assets amount to €175,000.

Requirement:
You are required to prepare a statement of financial position after the first year of trading.

Chapter 2

Evaluating Economic Relationships Using Accounting Ratios

Introduction

One of the most important functions of financial statements is to provide information about the economic performance and resources of the business entity. In addition to being able to examine the amounts of particular items in the financial statements the user can also look at both the relationships between different items in the financial statements and examine how they change over time. This process is one part of 'Financial Statement Analysis.'

It is very important that accounting ratios should be analysed in the context of the business entity. Ratios cannot give much insight into the economics of the firm if they are not interpreted very carefully. The factors that are important in the interpretation of accounting ratios are given below:

The Economics of the Firm's Industry

The relationships between the numbers in the financial statements depend on the economics of the firm's industry. Firms have different levels of profitability, different capital requirements and different links between profitability and assets. The main differences between companies are in terms of the type of assets they use and the types of cash inflow and outflows that they have. Some firms have mainly physical assets that can be capitalised in the statement of financial position. Other firms have few physical and mainly knowledge based assets. For example, CRH plc a manufacturer of concrete and building products has mainly physical assets while a more service orientated business like a business consultancy has few physical assets. In the case of the business consultancy, its main resources are the people that work for it. These peoples' ability to attract clients and provide services to them is the valuable resource. Accountancy recognises the values of these resources when they generate cash flows and sales.

Capitalization of assets

When a firm invests in assets that can yield future benefits they can either be capitalised in the statement of financial position and depreciated over the time period during which the asset benefits the firm or they can be expensed immediately in the income statement. In the case of some assets such as land and buildings there is a clear link between the investment in the asset and the future benefits that flow from that asset. This means that accountants are happy to capitalise such assets. However, the link between future benefits and current expenditure can be much harder to establish for investments such as Research and Development (R&D). For example, a manufacturing firm will have a high level of assets that qualify for capitalisation and these assets will appear on its statement of financial position. A software firm's investments will be in the generation of expertise and computer programs that are hard to value verifiably. These investments will be expensed as they occur rather than being capitalised in the statement of financial position. This has implications for the measurement of the firm's resources and profitability. The nature of a firm's assets can also indicate the kind of finance that is available to a firm. Providers of debt finance such as banks only advance loans to firms with sufficient physical assets to provide collateral in order to guarantee the loan.

Variable vs. fixed costs

It is also important to appreciate the differences between firms in term of their cost structures. Some firms have high levels of variable costs. These costs increase with each extra unit of production. For example, a manufacturing company will only incur the costs of raw materials for its products when it manufactures another unit. Fixed costs are costs that do not vary with the level of production. Examples of fixed costs would be items likes rent and to a certain extent employee wages. The profitability of high fixed costs firms will be highly dependent on the volume of business that they transact.

Cash cycle

Firms differ in the speed with which they can manufacture their product, sell the product, collect their debts and pay their suppliers. The connection between all of these activities is called the cash cycle.

A manufacturing firm will have a long cash cycle. It has to take deliver of raw materials in advance of manufacture. These raw materials must be paid for usually about 3 months later regardless of whether they have been used in the production process at that point. The firm then converts the raw materials into a finished product. The costs of this process such as wages and factory rent must be met as they are incurred. The finished product is then usually stored in a warehouse for a period of time. The product is then delivered to a customer. However, most manufacturing firms offer a credit period so they will not receive payment for 3 to 6 months. The full cash cycle may be from 6 months to a year for many manufacturing firms.

Other firms are in a more fortunate position in relation to their cash. Retail firms receive cash immediately from customers when they make a sale. They can also demand generous credit terms from their suppliers. In some cases, they have sold the goods before they have to pay for them and this means that they can invest the spare cash in the interim period. These investment returns can be an important source of profitability for some firms.

Analysis of Financial Statements

The firm's financial statements can be examined under a number of headings. These are Liquidity, Leverage, Profitability and Return on Investment.

Liquidity

Liquidity is the firm's ability to meet its short term obligations. Every business has to have enough cash to pay its various bills. These include wages, suppliers, tax and loan repayments. A business must plan its cash balances at the bank, its cash receipts from its customers and its cash payments such that it does not run out of cash. If the business does run out of cash it must negotiate a bank overdraft or a longer-term bank loan. This may enable the firm to recover. If the firm cannot get more cash then it may face liquidation, receivership or examinership. The usual sequence of events for a firm with liquidity problems is as follows. Firstly, the firm will have reduced cash inflows or increased cash outflows. This may have been caused by expansion of the firms business, disruption to the firm's production or slow payments from customers. Secondly, the situation may worsen when the firm finds it hard to pay its suppliers. These suppliers may cut off supplies of goods and services. If the firm's bank or its customers become aware of the situation then they may start to take action. The bank may refuse to advance future loans or increased overdraft facilities. Customers may find alternative suppliers and may even refuse to pay their bills if they think the firm may go out of business. Thirdly, if the firm runs out of cash it will be unable to pay bank loan repayments. Banks have usually taken security over the firm's main assets. They will appoint a receiver to sell these assets and give the proceeds back to the bank. These assets are usually the firm's land, buildings and machines and it is usually not possible for the firm to survive without them. Fourthly, the firm may then have to enter liquidation. This is a legal process where the firm's creditors appoint a liquidator to sell the firm's assets and distribute the proceeds to the creditors. In Ireland, a firm can also enter examinership. This is where the firm applies to have an examiner appointed by the courts. The Examiner runs the company until such time as it can continue its business or enter liquidation.

The firm's liquidity is accessed by looking at the firm's short term resources and the firm's short-term liabilities. These items are usually represented by current assets and current liabilities on the statement of financial position. The most obvious item to consider is the cash balance. If the firm has enough cash to pay its bills for a few months then it probably does not have a liquidity problem. However, if the firm has a large bank overdraft then it almost certainly has a liquidity problem. Stocks and debtors should be considered next. Receivables are a liquid asset in that we expect to receive cash from them in a short period of time. The firm can make efforts to receive cash more quickly by shortening credit terms, offering inducements for early payments and following up overdue accounts. Excessive pressure on customers to pay their debts can lead to lost sales and start rumours that the firm is in financial difficulty. Inventory can also be a source of cash. However, efforts to sell stock quickly may result in less cash because of discounts. Some stock cannot be sold quickly and is of little use in cash crises. On the liabilities side the main items to consider are creditors, taxation and loan repayments. Creditors are owed money by the firm. It is usually possible for the firm to delay payments to creditors and delay cash payments. If this strategy is taken too far the creditors may refuse to supply the firm or take legal action against the firm. Tax payments are due on specific dates and if the firm fails to make the payments they will be subject to interest charges and fines. Overdue loan repayments are the most difficult item to deal with for businesses with cash flow difficulties. When a firm takes out a long-term loan they agree to repay the loan and interest on particular dates. They also sign a loan agreement that gives the bank the right to take the firm's assets if the firm does not repay the loan as agreed. If the firm misses a loan payment then the bank may exercise its rights under this agreement.

Liquidity can be measured using a the ratios given in Figure 2.1

Figure 2.1
Liquidity Ratios

Current Ratio = Current Assets ÷ Current Liabilities *to 1*

Acid-test Ratio = (Current Assets – Inventory) ÷ Current Liabilities *to 1*

The current ratio shows the relationship between current assets and current liabilities. For example, if current assets are €100,000 and current liabilities are €50,000 then the current ratio is 2 to 1. This ratio indicates the relationship between short-term resources and short-term obligations.

If the ratio shows that short-term resources are equal to short-term obligations (current ratio = 1 to 1) then depending on the circumstances the firm may have a liquidity problem. In this case, it is very important to consider the context of the business before forming a conclusion. If the business has a long cash cycle then it has to invest resources in raw materials, manufacturing costs and storage costs and wait a long time before receiving cash for its finished goods. This puts a great deal of financial strain on the enterprise. If anything were to go wrong like production problems or a strike it would be very difficult for the business to continue with very little cash coming in. In this case, it is important that the business have an excess of current assets over current liabilities. This gives the firm a financial cushion against unexpected events. For this reason, investors use a rule-of-thumb of 2 to 1 for the current ratio for manufacturing firms.

When the current ratio falls below 2 to 1 many financial commentators assume that this indicates a liquidity problem. This is not necessarily the case. Many firms do not have a long cash cycle. For example, retail firms and airlines are in the more favourable position of receiving cash for their goods or services before they have to pay for the provision of the goods or service. Most airline flights are booked and paid-for in advance. This means the airline receives the cash but does not have to provide any services until the date of travel. The money generated from this effect is often invested in short-term investments in order to increase the profits of the airline. From a liquidity point of view, this means that money is coming into the business all the time. A liquidity problem is unlikely in these circumstances. That is not to say that the business could not have financial problems but they are less likely to be related to liquidity.

The acid-test ratio is another version of the current ratio. The only difference is that stock is excluded from current assets. This is because stock is an illiquid asset. In general, it cannot be sold quickly. Investors use a rule-of-thumb of 1 to 1 for the acid-test ratios of manufacturing firms. Like the current ratio the acid-test ratio can fall significantly below 1 to 1 without indicating liquidity problems for companies with a short cash cycle.

Leverage

Leverage is the amount the firm has borrowed relative to the amount of finance provided by the owners of the firm. Firms can obtain finance from two major sources. Firstly, firms can obtain finance from their owners. This is called equity capital. Owners provide equity in two main ways. They contribute equity directly by paying for their shares in the company and they contribute internally generated equity by not withdrawing profits from the firm. Secondly, firms can obtain long term finance from banks. Each of these sources of finance has implications for the risk profile and profitability of the firm.

Equity capital

The owners of the firm hold the issued share capital of the firm. They are also entitled to the residual of assets less liabilities. The issued share capital of the firm is permanent capital and the shareholders cannot demand its repayment. They are entitled to dividends but these dividends are at the discretion of the board of directors. If the firm goes into liquidation then shareholders rank last and will only receive money when all the other creditors have been paid. Shareholders do control the firm as they are entitled to elect the board of directors.

In summary equity capital does not have to be repaid and dividend payments do not have to be made if the firm does not have adequate resources. This means equity capital is very safe for the firm. However, holding shares in the firm is risky for the shareholders. They have no guarantees as to future dividend payments or shares prices. If the firm encounters financial difficulties then there is unlikely to be anything left for the shareholders. If the firm does well and created extra value then most of that extra value will accrue to the shareholders as they are entitled to the residual value of the firm.

Debt capital

Debt capital is capital provided to the firm by banks or other financial institutions. The bank and the firm enter into a loan agreement whereby the bank advances the money to the firm in exchange for a number of repayments on specific dates. These repayments will cover the repayment of both the original amount advanced and interest at an agreed rate.

Taking on debt is more risky for businesses than financing using equity. If the business does not keep up its agreed repayments on its borrowings it could be forced into receivership, bankruptcy or liquidation. This means that large levels of debt are only suitable for businesses that have the ability to repay the debt. Businesses with healthy profits and cash flows are good candidates for higher levels of debt. For example, CRH plc has very steady cash flows from its business. This makes it a good candidate for borrowing. Businesses that have very uncertain cash flows are not good candidates for debt. High technology firms tend to finance mainly from equity and do not use debt at all.

When banks review loan applications from businesses they have two main criteria in mind. Firstly, does the business have sufficient profits and cash flow to repay the debt? Banks access this by looking the businesses financial statements for a number of years. Secondly, does the business have sufficient security or collateral for the debt? Security refers to assets that can be sold by the bank if the company fails to repay the loan. Land and buildings and other physical assets are considered good security by banks.

Taking on debt has an advantage over equity in that banks only get paid back their capital and interest and do not share in the residual value of the firm. This means that shareholders can increase their returns by including more debt in the businesses capital structure. For example, suppose Lever plc has profits of €100 and equity of €1,000. This means that it is earning a return of 10% (€100/€1,000) on its equity. Now suppose Lever has the chance to expand its business but requires an extra €1,000 of funding. This expansion will provide extra profits of €100. Assume the interest rate is 5%. Table 2.1 shows the calculation of return on equity for this firm.

Table 2.1

	Original firm	**Expansion financed by equity**	**Expansion financed by debt**
Profits	€100	€200	€200
Less interest (€1,000 x 5%)			(€50)
Profits after interest	€100	€200	€150
Equity	€1,000	€2,000	€1,000
Debt			€1,000
Total finance	€1,000	€2,000	€2,000
Return on equity	10%	10%	15%
	€100/€1,000	€200/€2,000	€150/€1,000

This example shows that Lever plc has increased returns to its shareholders from 10% to 15% by taking on debt rather than equity. This works because the shareholders get to keep all the profits of the firm after all expenses (including interest) have been paid. In this case the extra profit from the expansion is €100. The bank charges interest of €50 so €50 of extra profit is generated for the shareholders even though they have not put any extra funds into the business. This process is called 'trading on the equity.' The extra return has to be balanced against the extra risk that the shareholders have introduced into their business. If the business were not able to pay back the loan to the bank then the shareholders could lose all of their investment in the business.

Leverage is measured using the debt-equity percentage. This is the amount of non-current loans and borrowings divided by the total equity. The formula for the Debt/Equity percentage is given in Figure 2.2.

Figure 2.2
Leverage Measure

Debt/Equity percentage = Non-Current Loans and Borrowings ÷ Total Equity %

Different businesses have different levels of debt. This depends on the circumstances of their business and the environment in which they operate. Table 2.2 summaries the characteristics of high debt and low debt businesses.

Table 2.2

High debt businesses	Low debt businesses
High levels of assets that can be used as security	Low levels of assets suitable for security
Steady profits and cash flows that can be used to repay debt	Volatile profits (or loss making)
Non-cyclical industry	Cyclical industry
Invests in low risk projects that provide cash flows quickly (e.g. new factory to produce an existing product)	Invests in high risk projects like oil exploration and R&D.

Firms will select the amount of debt that they take on with regard to these factors.

Profitability

Profitability is the amount of profit that the business is generating from its operations. The amount of profit that can be generated depends on many factors. These include the amount of competition in the industry, the costs of providing the goods or services and the mix between fixed and variable costs. Figure 2.3 shows the two main measures of profitability that are commonly used.

Figure 2.3
Profitability Measures

Gross Profit Percentage = Gross Profit ÷ Revenue %

Net Profit Percentage = Profit Before Finance Costs ÷ Revenue %

The gross profit percentage shows how much profit has been generated after subtracting the costs of making or buying in the firm's products. The gross profit percentage does not take account of any distribution, marketing or administrative costs. Neither does it take account of interest or taxes. The gross profit percentage is often used a measure of the core profitability of the business. In most businesses it remains stable over long periods of time. The gross profit percentage can be compared to the same percentage for other firms in the same industry without difficulty.

The gross profit percentage does vary widely for different businesses. The percentage depends on the economics of the business. For most manufacturing businesses the costs of making their products may account for 70% of their sales revenue. For other businesses such as an advertising agency cost of goods sold may only account for 5-10% of its sales.

The net profit percentage measures the amount of profit generated after paying all the costs of the business excluding interest and taxes. It is a measure of how much profit is being generated for each euro of sales. Table 2.2 shows the calculation of the gross profit percentage and the net profit percentage for ABC plc.

Table 2.2

ABC plc Income Statement
for the financial year ended 31st December 2006

	€
Revenue	200,000
Cost of sales	(150,00)
Gross profit	50,000
Operating costs	(35,000)
Group operating profit	15,000
Finance costs	(3,000)
Profit before tax	12,000
Income tax expense	(1,400)
Group profit for the financial year	10,560
Gross profit % (€50,000/€200,000)	25%
Net profit % (€15,000/€200,000)	7.5%

Return on Investment

Return on investment compares the profits that have been generated with the investment that required for the business. The return on equity percentage compares the profit that has been generated for the shareholders to their investment in the business. The profit available to the shareholders is always measured after interest[18]. The shareholders' investment in the business is measured as the total equity in the company. The return that is calculated from this formula can be compared to the return shareholders would make by investing in other companies or putting their money in a bank. This percentage measures the return to the shareholders alone. It is often higher than the return on capital employed due to the effect of leverage on returns. Return on capital employed is the return on all of the investment in the business. This includes both the shareholders' investment and any funds that the company has borrowed. The profit to be used in this percentage is profit before finance costs. This is because finance costs the return to the banks that have lent money to the company. Capital employed is calculated as non-current liabilities plus total equity. This includes funds received from both shareholders and

[18] It may be calculated either before or after tax. All of the formulas in this chapter are calculated before tax. The logic of excluding tax is that it is determined by tax rules and not under the control of the management of the business.

banks. Return on assets shows the returns generated on the businesses assets. The formulas for these percentages are given in Figure 2.4 below:

Figure 2.4
Return on Investment Measures

Return on Equity = Profit Before Tax ÷ Total Equity %

Return on Capital Employed =

Profit Before Finance Costs ÷ Capital Employed* %

Return on Assets = Profit Before Finance Costs ÷ Total Assets %

*Capital Employed = Total Non-Current Liabilities + Total Equity

For example, suppose Return plc generated profit after tax of €100, has interest charges of €20, non-current liabilities of €600 and total equity of €1,000. The calculation of return on equity and return on capital employed would be as follows:

Table 2.3

	ABC plc
Profit before finance costs	€100
Less interest	(20)
Profits before tax	€80
Equity	€1,000
Debt	600
Total finance	€1,600

Return on equity		
= Profit before tax	€80	= 8%
Total equity	€1,000	
Return on capital employed		
= Profit before finance costs	€100	= 6.25%
Non-current Liabilities + total equity	€1,600	

Operational performance measures

Accounting information can also be used to provide some information on the efficiency with which the business is being run. Non-current asset turnover shows how efficiently the business is generating sales from its non-current assets. Receivables days and payables days show how quickly the business is receiving cash from its customers and paying cash to its suppliers. These figures will usually be in the 30-90 day range but will depend on the business and the kind of credit terms offered. Inventory days show how quickly the business is selling its inventory. This depends on the business. A jewellery shop might expect to hold goods in inventory for 6 months while grocery stores sell most of the inventory in a matter of days. The definitions of the operational performance measures are given in Figure 2.5 below.

Figure 2.5
Operational Performance Measures

Non-current Asset Turnover = Revenue ÷ Non-current Assets *(Times)*

Inventory percentage = Average Inventory* ÷ Cost of Goods Sold %

Inventory days = (Average Inventory x 365) ÷ Cost of Goods Sold *(days)*

Receivables days = (Receivables x 365) ÷ Credit Sales Revenue** *(days)*

Payables days = (Payables x 365) ÷ Credit Purchases*** *(days)*

** Average Inventory = (Beginning Inventory + Ending Inventory)/2*
If average inventory is not available then use closing inventory
*** If credit sales revenue is not available then use sales revenue*
**** If credit purchases are not available then use cost of goods sold.*

Summary

Information contained in the income statement and statement of financial position can be used to construct new measures called accounting ratios. These ratios combine accounting information to provide more information about the business. Liquidity measures show whether the business is able to pay its short term debts. Leverage measures show how much money the business has borrowed relative to the amount provided by shareholders. Profitability and return measures show how much profit and return is being generated by the business.

Chapter 2 Exercises

Exercise 2.1

Murphy Machine Tools Ltd.
Statement of Financial Position
as at 31st December, 20x6

	€'000	€'000
Non-current assets		
Property, plant and equipment		3,732
Current assets		
Inventory	450	
Receivables	1,012	
Bank	245	
		1,707
Total assets		5,439
Equity		
Equity share capital (shares of €1 each)		1,000
Retained income		3,109
		4,109
Non-current liabilities		
Long term loans		651
Current liabilities		
Payables	342	
Corporation tax	103	
Accruals	234	
		679
Total equity and liabilities		5,439

Murphy Machine Tools Ltd.
Income Statement
for the year ended 31st December, 20x6

	20x6
	€'000
Revenue	4,523
Cost of sales	3,106
Gross profit	1,417
Operating costs	432
Operating profit	985
Profit on disposal of non-current assets	10
Profit before finance costs	995
Finance costs	52
Profit before taxation	943
Income taxation expense	97
Profit for the financial year	846

Other Information: -

Murphy Machine Tools Ltd. is an Engineering company. It manufactures parts for machine tools that are sold to multinational companies in the UK and US. Its main factory is in Cork. Jim Murphy owns all of the shares. He is chairman of the board and chief executive. Murphy Machine Tools Ltd paid dividends of €100,000 during the year and a final dividend of €234,000 was proposed.

Required:

(1) Analyse the performance of Murphy Machine Tools Ltd. using the following ratios: -

(a) Current ratio;
(b) Acid-test ratio;
(c) Debt-equity percentage;
(d) Return on capital employed;
(e) Return on equity;
(f) Gross profit percentage;
(g) Inventory days;
(h) Receivables days;
(i) Payables days;

(2) Discuss the profitability, liquidity and leverage of Murphy Machine Tools Ltd. Support your answer using appropriate ratios from the list above.

Exercise 2.2

Irish Metal Cases Limited

Statement of financial position information as at 31st December 20x6.

	€'000
Property, plant and equipment	29,921
Inventory	2,045
Receivables	3,219
Bank	12
Short-term bank loans and overdrafts	613
Trade and other payables	4,567
Long-term loans	8,309
Equity share capital (shares of €1 each)	1,200
Share premium account	12,163
Retained income	8,345

Irish Metal Cases Ltd.
Income Statement
for the year ended 31st December, 20x6

	20x6	20x5
	€'000	€'000
Revenue	20,132	16,754
Cost of sales	12,079	10,890
Gross profit	8,053	5,864
Operating costs	6,432	4,345
Operating profit	1,621	1,519
Profit on disposal of non-current assets	10	7
Profit before finance costs	1,631	1,526
Finance costs	840	780
Profit before taxation	791	746
Taxation expense	323	234
Profit for the financial year	468	512

Other Information: -

Irish Metal Cases Ltd. is a Light Engineering company. It manufactures cases for personal computers that are sold to multinational computer companies. Its main factory is in Galway. The Murphy family owns all of the shares. James Murphy is chairman of the board and chief executive.

Required:

(1) Analyse the performance of Irish Metal Cases Ltd. using the following ratios: -

- (a) Current ratio;
- (b) Acid-test ratio;
- (c) Debt-equity percentage;
- (d) Return on capital employed;
- (e) Return on equity;
- (f) Gross profit percentage;
- (g) Inventory turnover;
- (h) Receivables days;
- (i) Payables days;

(2) Discuss the profitability and liquidity of Irish Metal Cases Ltd. Support your answer using appropriate ratios from the list above.

Exercise 2.3

Irish Software Ltd.
Statement of financial position as at 31st December 20x6

	€'000	€'000
Non-current assets		
Property, plant and equipment		1,230
Current assets		
Debtors	3,512	
Cash	10,134	
		13,646
Total assets		14,876
Equity		
Equity share capital (shares of €1 each)		400
Retained income		8,009
		8,409
Non-current liabilities		
Long term loans		5,208
Current liabilities		
Bank loans and overdrafts	154	
Trade and other creditors	208	
Corporation tax	897	
		1,259
Total equity and liabilities		14,876

Irish Software Ltd.
Income statement for the year ended 31st December

	20x6	20x5
	€'000	€'000
Revenue	30,840	20,145
Cost of sales	14,079	10,890
Gross profit	16,761	9,255
Operating costs	8,296	8,100
Profit before finance costs	8,465	1,155
Finance costs	500	251
Profit before taxation	7,965	904
Taxation expense	801	87
Profit for the financial year	7,164	817

Other Information: -

Irish Software Ltd. is a computer software company based in Dublin. It was founded about ten years ago by four computer programmers. They each own 25% of the shares in the company. Over the last two years the company has been extremely successful. It develops and sells software that helps to secure computer systems.

Required:

(1) Calculate the following ratios for Irish Software Ltd.: -

(a) Current ratio;
(b) Debt-equity percentage;
(c) Return on capital employed;
(d) Return on equity;
(e) Gross profit percentage;
(f) Receivables days;
(g) Payables days;

(2) Discuss the profitability and gearing of Irish Software Ltd. Support your answer using appropriate ratios from the list above.

Exercise 2.4

Saw-it plc and Hammer-down plc are two Irish companies that each has a chain of DIY stores. Their Income Statements for 2005, selected data from their statements of financial position and their common size statements are given below:

Table 1

Income statement for the year ended 31st December, 2005	**Saw-it 2005 €'000**	**Hammer-down 2005 €'000**
Revenue	42,523	31,200
Cost of sales	29,106	23,400
Gross profit	13,417	7,800
Operating costs	8,600	4,300
Operating profit	4,817	3,500
Profit on disposal of fixed assets	-	500
Profit before finance costs	4,817	4,000
Finance costs	1,200	120
Profit before taxation	3,617	3,880
Taxation	480	470
Profit for the financial year	3,137	3,410

Table 2

Statement of financial position (selected items) as at 31st December 2005	**Saw-it 2005 €'000**	**Hammer-down 2005 €'000**
Inventory	3,600	2,300
Non-current debt	20,000	2,000
Equity	5,000	18,000

Table 3

Common size statements (based on revenue)	**Saw-it**	**Hammer-down**
	2005	**2005**
	€'000	**€'000**
Revenue	100.00%	100.00%
Cost of sales	68.45%	75.00%
Gross profit	31.55%	25.00%
Operating costs	20.22%	13.78%
Operating profit	11.33%	11.22%
Profit on disposal of fixed assets	-	1.60%
Profit before finance costs	11.33%	12.82%
Finance costs	2.82%	0.38%
Profit before taxation	8.51%	12.44%
Taxation	1.13%	1.51%
Profit for the financial year	7.38%	10.93%

REQUIRED:

(1) Analyze and compare the profitability of Saw-it and Hammer-down.

(2) Calculate the following percentages for both companies

- Return on equity
- Return on capital employed

Analyze and compare these percentages for Saw-it and Hammer-down.

(3) Briefly describe and explain the type of information required in order to access the liquidity of a company.

Chapter 3

Recording Basic Transactions

Introduction

We have seen that the primary objective of financial statements is to provide information about the performance and resources of a business to a wide variety of users. In order to fulfil this objective the accounting system must record the transactions of the business systematically. The accounting system must also provide a way of classifying and summarising these transactions in a way that will provide useful information to the users of financial statements.

The Accounting Equation and Recording Transactions

The way in which transactions are recorded in the accounting system is governed by the accounting equation. This equation determines the relationships between assets, liabilities and equity. Each time a transaction occurs it must be recorded in a way that keeps the accounting equation in balance.

Figure 3.1
The Accounting Equation

Assets – Liabilities = Equity

Let's take some example transactions and look at their impact on the accounting equation.

Example 1
Suppose that Ms. Murphy has just set up a limited company and wants to invest €1,000 in the company. She will write a personal cheque for €1,000 to the company. This cheque will be lodged to the company's bank account and she will receive 1,000 shares of €1.00 each. After this transaction has been completed how has the accounting equation for the company (Murphy's Muffins Ltd.) changed? The company had now got more assets because the bank account has gone from €0.00 to €1,000.00 (remember the company has just been set up). What else has changed? The company has issued 1,000 shares

so its issued share capital has gone up by 1,000 shares by €1.00, or €1,000. In this case the increase in the assets of the company has been exactly offset by an increase in the equity of the company.

Table 3.1

	Before any shares issued €	**Issue of 1,000 shares €**	**After Issue of Shares €**
Assets			
Bank	0.00	+1,000	1,000
Equity			
Issued share capital	0.00	+1,000	1,000
Shares of €1.00 each			

We need a systematic way to record this transaction and all of the other transactions into which the business enters. This system is called 'Double-Entry Bookkeeping.' The idea is to use the special words 'Debit' and 'Credit' to indicate increases and decreases in the items that make up the accounting equation. This convention is used throughout accounting and means that accountants can understand each other's work.

Debit is defined as an increase in an asset or a decrease in a liability or an equity item. Credit is defined as an increase in a liability or an equity item or a decrease in an asset. These definitions are summarised in the following table.

Table 3.2

	Debit	**Credit**
Increase in	An asset	A liability or equity item
Decrease in	A liability or equity item	An asset

Using this table we can write down how the above transaction can be recorded using the double-entry system. The bank will be debited because this is an asset account and it has increased. The issued share capital will be credited because this is an equity item and it has increased. The full transaction looks like this

Table 3.3 Journal entry to record issue of share capital

Date	Account	Debit	Credit
...	Bank	1,000	
...	Issued share capital		1,000

Being issue of share capital to Ms. Murphy

Table 3.3 is called a 'Journal Entry.' It is the effect of a particular transaction on the balances in the various accounts that make up the business's financial records. It is important to notice a few things about this journal entry.

Firstly, the total of the 'debits' in a journal entry must always be equal to the total of the 'credits.' This is in order to keep the accounting equation in balance. If you debited an asset the asset would increase. Another asset has to decrease or a liability or equity item has to increase in order to keep the accounting equation in balance.

Secondly, the journal entry is presented in a certain format. The accounts to be debited or credited are listed in the account column (debits first) and the amounts that are to be debited or credited to each account are listed in the 'Debit' and 'Credit' columns. This presentation makes it each to see that the 'debits' and 'credits' add up and that this transaction will keep the accounting equation in balance.

Finally, a brief description of the transaction is written underneath the journal entry. This means that anybody interested in why this transaction was recorded can quickly see to what it relates.

Example 2

Murphy's Muffins Ltd. decides to purchase a Muffin-Maker for €500. This transaction involves the company writing a cheque to the manufacturer of the Muffin-Maker and receiving the machine in exchange. How does this transaction effect the accounting equation? The bank will decrease by €500 and a new account will be set up for the machine and increased by €500.

Table 3.4

	Before Machine Purchased €	**Machine Purchase €**	**After Machine Purchased €**
Assets			
Machine		+500	500
Bank	1,000	-500	500
Equity			
Issued share capital	1,000		1,000
Shares of €1.00 each			

How will this transaction be recorded using the double-entry bookkeeping system? Bank has decreased so it will be credited (refer back to Table 3.2). We now have a new asset (the machine) so the machine account will be debited.

Table 3.5 Journal entry to record purchase of machine

Date	**Account**	**Debit**	**Credit**
...	Machine	500	
...	Bank		500

Being acquisition of new Muffin-Making machine.

Example 3

The directors of Murphy's Muffins realise that they need more money to run their business so they approach their bank manager for a loan. The bank manager agrees to give them a loan of €1,500 to expand their business. One effect of this transaction is to increase our bank account when we receive the loan. The other effect is that we have to record a liability to the bank for the amount of the loan. In other word the bank asset has increased and this increase is matched by an increase in a bank loan liability.

Table 3.6

	Before Bank Loan €	Bank Loan €	After Bank Loan €
Assets			
Machine	500		500
Bank	500	+1,500	2,000
Liabilities			
Bank loan	0	+1,500	1,500
Equity			
Issued share capital	1,000		1,000
Shares of €1.00 each			

This transaction would be recorded as follows using the double-entry system. The bank asset would be debited to reflect the increase in our bank account and the bank loan account would be credited to reflect our liability to the bank.

Table 3.7 Journal entry to record receipt of bank loan

Date	Account	Debit	Credit
...	Bank (asset a/c)	1,500	
...	Bank loan (liability a/c)		1,500

Being receipt of bank loan.

Keeping Track of Transactions

These examples show an important aspect of the accounting system. That is, the effect of transactions is cumulative. You change the accounts for one transaction (say the purchase of the machine) and then move onto the next transaction (the bank loan). We need a systematic method of keeping track of the effects of these transactions on the accounts that make up the assets, liabilities and equity of the business. The method that was used in the days of manual bookkeeping was called the 'T Account System.' It is important to understand how this system works because it has been transferred to computer systems where most bookkeeping tasks are now carried out.

The T Account system works as follows. Each asset, liability or equity item is given its own T Account. In the manual system this consisted of about a half page of ruled paper with a red line down the middle. For example, the bank account would have had its own T account. The left hand side of the T account is designated as debit and the right hand side is designated as credit. When a transaction occurs, a journal entry is written down for that transaction. Then the transaction is entered in the T Accounts. This is done by recording the debits for an account on the left hand side of that accounts page and recording the credit affecting that account on the right hand page.

Table 3.8 A 'T Account'

Debit		**Bank**			**Credit**
Date	*Account*	*Amount*	*Date*	*Account*	*Amount*

Table 3.8 shows an example T Account. The name of the account to which the T Account relates is given at the top of the 'T Account.' In this case it is the 'Bank' T Account. This means that all of the debits and credits that relate to the Bank account will appear in this T Account. Debit is marked on the left hand side of the T Account. All of the debit entries to the bank account will appear on this side. All of the credit entries will appear on the other side.

Using T Accounts to Record Transactions

Earlier in the chapter we developed three journal entries that record three specific transactions. We will now use 'T Accounts' to record these transactions.

The first transaction's journal entry was as follows:

Table 3.9 Journal entry to record issue of share capital

Date	**Account**	**Debit**	**Credit**
...	Bank	1,000	
...	Issued share capital		1,000
Being issue of share capital to Ms. Murphy			

We will record this transaction in the 'Bank' T Account and the 'Issued Share Capital' T Account.

Table 3.10

Debit **Bank** **Credit**

Date	*Account*	*Amount*	*Date*	*Account*	*Amount*
...	Issued share capital	1,000			

Debit **Issued Share Capital** **Credit**

Date	*Account*	*Amount*	*Date*	*Account*	*Amount*
			...	Bank	1,000

The debit to the bank account is shown on the debit side of the bank T Account and the credit to issued share capital is show on the credit side of the issued share capital account. Note that the name of the corresponding account is written beside the entry. For example, in the bank account we write 'Issued Share Capital' beside the debit entry of €1,000. This makes T Accounts easy to read and to understand.

The second transaction related to the purchase of a machine and was recorded as follows:

Table 3.11 Journal entry to record purchase of machine

Date	**Account**	**Debit**	**Credit**
...	Machine	500	
...	Bank		500

Being acquisition of new Muffin-Making machine.

This transaction will be recorded in the T Accounts as follows:

Table 3.12

Debit — **Bank** — **Credit**

Date	*Account*	*Amount*	*Date*	*Account*	*Amount*
...	Issued share capital	1,000	...	Machine	500

Debit — **Machine** — **Credit**

Date	*Account*	*Amount*	*Date*	*Account*	*Amount*
...	Bank	500			

Debit — **Issued Share Capital** — **Credit**

Date	*Account*	*Amount*	*Date*	*Account*	*Amount*
			...	Bank	1,000

The third transaction relates to taking out a bank loan. Its journal entry was as follows:

Table 3.13 Journal entry to record receipt of bank loan

Date	**Account**	**Debit**	**Credit**
...	Bank (asset a/c)	1,500	
...	Bank loan (liability a/c)		1,500

Being receipt of bank loan.

This transaction is reflected in the T Accounts by debiting the bank T Account and crediting the bank loan T Account.

Table 3.14

Debit — **Bank** — **Credit**

Date	*Account*	*Amount*	*Date*	*Account*	*Amount*
...	Issued share capital	1,000	...	Machine	500
...	***Bank Loan***	***1,500***			

Debit — **Machine** — **Credit**

Date	*Account*	*Amount*	*Date*	*Account*	*Amount*
...	Bank	500			

Debit — **Bank Loan** — **Credit**

Date	*Account*	*Amount*	*Date*	*Account*	*Amount*
			...	***Bank***	***1,500***

Debit — **Issued Share Capital** — **Credit**

Date	*Account*	*Amount*	*Date*	*Account*	*Amount*
			...	Bank	1,000

Table 3.14 shows the T Accounts after recording the three transactions. Have a look at the bank account. You can see what happened to the bank account during the period just by looking at this account. The company received cash in exchange for issued share capital, it spent some cash on an asset and it received a bank loan.

To summarise, each T Account contains all of the transactions that affect that account for the period under consideration.

Balancing the T Accounts

We can now work out the cumulative effect of all of the transactions in a particular T Account by 'Balancing the Account'. This procedure is carried out as follows:

1. Add up both the debit side and credit side of the account and write the total of the larger side at the bottom of each column.

2. Write in the balance to be carried forward on the smaller side of the T Account.

3. Transfer that amount down to the opposite side.

For example, we add up each side of the bank account. The debit side totals €2,500 and the credit side total €500, so we write €2,500 (the larger amount) under each of the columns.

Table 3.15

Debit		**Bank**			**Credit**
Date	*Account*	*Amount*	*Date*	*Account*	*Amount*
...	Issued share capital	1,000	...	Machine	500
...	Bank loan	1,500			
		2,500			2,500

Now we enter the balance on the smaller side of the T Account. The balance is the total of the larger side less the total of the smaller side. In this case, this is €2,500 less €500, which equals €2,000. This is entered at the bottom of the T Account on the smaller side.

Table 3.16

Debit		**Bank**			**Credit**
Date	*Account*	*Amount*	*Date*	*Account*	*Amount*
...	Issued share capital	1,000	...	Machine	500
...	Bank loan	1,500			
				Balance	2,000
		2,500			2,500
	Balance	2,000			

This procedure may seem cumbersome but its effect is simply to add up the debits and the credits and put the net balance on the correct side. In this account, there were €2,500 of debits and €500 of credits, so the net balance is €2,000 debit. This is what is shown on the above account, a balance of €2,000 on the debit side. Table 3.17 shows the balances on each of the T Accounts.

Table 3.17

Bank

Debit			Credit		
Date	*Account*	*Amount*	*Date*	*Account*	*Amount*
...	Issued share capital	1,000	...	Machine	500
...	Bank Loan	1,500			
				Balance	2,000
		2,500			2,500
	Balance	2,000			

Machine

Debit			Credit		
Date	*Account*	*Amount*	*Date*	*Account*	*Amount*
...	Bank	500		Balance	500
		500			500
	Balance	500			

Bank Loan

Debit			Credit		
Date	*Account*	*Amount*	*Date*	*Account*	*Amount*
	Balance	1,500	...	Bank	1,500
		1,500			1,500
				Balance	1,500

Issued Share Capital

Debit			Credit		
Date	*Account*	*Amount*	*Date*	*Account*	*Amount*
	Balance	1,000	...	Bank	1,000
		1,000			1,000
				Balance	1,000

Extracting a Trial Balance

We can now easily extract the balances from the T Accounts and prepare a 'Trial Balance.' This document lists down the accounts and the balances on those accounts.

Table 3.18
Trial Balance

Account	**Debit**	**Credit**
Bank	2,000	
Machine	500	
Bank loan		1,500
Issued share capital		1,000
	2,500	2,500

Each account is listed with the balance. This statement shows how the debits and credits have accumulated in each account. In general, assets will have a debit balance and liabilities and equity will have a credit balance. This is because each time an asset increases it is debited. This means that Table 3.19 can be used to identify which items are assets and liabilities on a trial balance.

Table 3.19

Balance	**Debit**	**Credit**
Type of account On Trial Balance	An asset	A liability or equity item

The trial balance should balance. This means that the debit column should add up to the same amount as the credit column. This is because in order to keep the accounting equation in balance there should be a debit for every credit.

Summary

We have covered a lot of ground in this chapter. Firstly, we saw that each transaction must be recorded in a way which is consistent with the accounting equation. Secondly, the double entry bookkeeping system was introduced. This system allows us to talk about increases and decreases in assets, liabilities and equity in terms of debits and credits. This enabled us to write each transaction down as a journal entry. Thirdly, we saw how transactions can be accumulated in T Accounts and how the T accounts can be balanced to give a Trial Balance.

Chapter 3 Exercises

Exercise 3.1

Fill in the missing entries in the following table:

	Debit	Credit
Increase in	ASSETS	LIABILITIES + EQUITIES
Decrease in	LIABILITIES + EQUITIES	ASSETS

Exercise 3.2

Ms. Beancounter started a new business by forming a limited company Beancounter Ltd. Her first 3 transactions are given below.

Transaction Number	Date	Description
1	1 Jan	Beancounter Ltd. is formed as a limited company and Ms. Beancounter invests €1,000 for 1,000 shares of €1 each
2	1 Jan	Beancounter Ltd. receives a loan of €500 from the Bank of Dublin. This amount is received immediately into Beancounter Ltd.'s bank account.
3	2 Jan	Beancounter Ltd. buys a second hand van for €1,000 and pays by cheque.

(a) Prepare the statement of financial position of Beancounter Ltd. as at the 2nd of January. Use the following table to trace through the transactions.

	Tx. 1	Tx. 2	Tx. 3	Statement of financial position as at 2nd January
Assets				
Van			1000	
Bank		500		
=				1500
Equity				
Issued share capital Shares of €1.00 each	1000			
+ Liabilities				
Bank loan		500		
				1500

(b) Prepare journal entries for each of the transactions

Tx. 1

Date	Account	Debit	Credit
1 JAN	ISSUED SHARE CAPITAL	1000	
1 "	ISSUED SHARE CAPITAL		1000

Being

Tx. 2

Date	Account	Debit	Credit
1 JAN	BANK	500	
1 JAN	BANK LOAN		500

Being

Tx. 3

Date	Account	Debit	Credit
2 JAN	VAN		1000
2 JAN	VAN	1000	

Being

(c) Post each of the journal entries to T accounts using the template below. Balance each T account.

Debit **Bank** **Credit**

Date	*Account*	*Amount*	*Date*	*Account*	*Amount*
1/1	CASH	500	2/1	VAN	1000
1/1	SHARE	1000			
			1/1	BALANCE	500
		1500			1500
1/1	BALANCE	500			

Debit **Van** **Credit**

Date	*Account*	*Amount*	*Date*	*Account*	*Amount*
2/1	VAN	1000	2/1	BALANCE	1000
		1000			1000
2/1	BALANCE	1000			

Debit **Bank Loan** **Credit**

Date	*Account*	*Amount*	*Date*	*Account*	*Amount*
2/1	BALANCE	500	2/1	LOAN	500
		500			500
			2/1	BALANCE	500

Debit **Issued Share Capital** **Credit**

Date	*Account*	*Amount*	*Date*	*Account*	*Amount*
1/2	BALANCE	1000	1/2	ISSUED	1000
			1/2	BALANCE	1000

(d) Extract a trial balance from the T accounts

Trial Balance

Account	**Debit**	**Credit**
Bank	500	
Van	1000	
Bank loan		500
Issued share capital		1000
	1500	1500

Chapter 4

Recording Revenue and Expenses using the Double Entry System

Introduction

In the last chapter the double entry bookkeeping system was introduced. However, only transactions affecting the statement of financial position were dealt with. The system will be extended to deal with transactions involving the income statement in this chapter.

The Income Statement

The statement of financial position shows the assets, liabilities and equities of the business. This lines up directly with the accounting equation

Figure 4.1
The Accounting Equation

Assets – Liabilities = Equity

The statement of financial position shows the amounts of assets, liabilities and equities at a point in time. For example, the bank asset should show the amount in the businesses bank account at the statement of financial position date. The income statement shows the movement in the equity during the year. The change in equity due to trading and operations is called 'Profit.'

Figure 4.2
The Accounting Equation

Assets – Liabilities = Opening Equity + Profit for the Year

where

Closing Equity = Opening Equity + Profit for the Year

The income statement shows all of the income and expense items that the business earned or incurred during the period. Sales revenues, deposit interest earned and rents earned are examples of revenues. These items usually cause assets to increase or liabilities to decrease. For example, a cash sale results in more cash in the bank which is an increase in an asset. This increase in an asset must be balanced by another change in the statement of financial position. In this case, it is an increase in retained income. The cash sale has increased the assets of the business and this is reflected in the equity of the business increasing. However, the retained income account is not increased directly because of this cash sale. All of the income and expense items are aggregated in the income statement and the profit figure (which equals income minus expenses) is added to retained income at the end of the accounting period. If all of the accounting is carried out correctly then adding the profit figure to retained income should 'balance' the statement of financial position.

Expenses are items like the cost of supplies, wages, light, heat, telephone bills and many other items. These items cause a decrease in assets or an increase in liabilities. For example, if a business receives and pays a telephone bill this will reduce the bank account by the amount of the telephone bill. This is matched with a decrease in the retained income account in the equity section of the statement of financial position.

Figure 4.3
The Income Statement

Profit = Income - Expenses

For example, take the statement of financial position of Murphy's Muffins at the end of the second month of trading and the third month of trading.

Table 4.1 Murphy's Muffins Ltd. Statement of Financial Position as at:

	31 January Year 1	28 February Year 1
Assets		
Machine	500	500
Bank	2,000	2,500
Liabilities		
Bank loan	(1,500)	(1,500)
	1,000	1,500
Equity		
Issued share capital	1,000	1,000
	1,000	?

Notice that the bank account has increased from €2,000 at the end of January to €2,500 at the end of February and everything else has stayed the same. Let's suppose this is because Murphy's Muffins bought ingredients for Muffins for €500 and sold the finished Muffins for €1,000. Let's also suppose there were no other costs or expenses during the month. What has happened is that Murphy's Muffins has €500 extra in the bank due to generating a profit during the month. How can we balance the statement of financial position in this situation? We introduce a new account called 'Retained Income.' This account contains the cumulative profit of the business to date.

Table 4.2 Murphy's Muffins Ltd. Statement of Financial Position at:

	31 January Year 1	28 February Year 1
Assets		
Machine	500	500
Bank	2,000	2,500
Liabilities		
Bank loan	(1,500)	(1,500)
	1,000	1,500
Equity		
Issued share capital	1,000	1,000
Retained income		500
	1,000	1,500

Investors and other users of Financial Statements would be interested in analysing the reason why retained income has increased to €500. The Income Statement meets this need. Table 4.3 shows what the Income Statement would look like in this simple situation.

Table 4.3 Murphy's Muffins Ltd. Income Statement for the period ended:

	28 February Year 1
Revenue	1,000
Cost of sales	(500)
Profit for the financial period	500

The profit for each financial period is added onto the retained income account in the statement of financial position in order to update the businesses equity for any profits that have been made during the period.

The retained income account in the balance sheet reflects the accumulated profits[19] of the entity since it was formed. For example, suppose that Murphy's Muffins made a profit of €1,000 for Year 2. Its income statement is shown in Table 4.4 and the equity section of its balance sheet is shown in Table 4.5. Retained income at the end of year 2 is €1,500. This is retained income at the end of year 1 (€500) plus the profit for year 2 (€1,000).

Table 4.4 Murphy's Muffins Ltd. Income Statement for the period ended:

	28 February Year 2
Revenue	2,000
Cost of sales	(1,000)
Profit for the financial period	1,000

Table 4.5 Murphy's Muffins Ltd. Statement of Financial Position at:

	28 February Year 2	**28 February Year 1**
Equity		
Issued share capital	1,000	1,000
Retained income	1,500	500
	2,500	1,500

Each year the retained income account is update by adding on the profit for that financial period to the balance on the retained income account from last year's statement of financial position.

[19] Dividends and certain other adjustments are also subtracted from the retained income account.

Equity and Profit

The definition of equity is "the residual interest in the assets of the entity after deducting all its liabilities." Equity is also the shareholders investment in the business and is owed back to the shareholders. If the firm were liquidated and all the assets had to be sold off and liabilities settled anything that was left would go to the shareholders. Therefore, when the firm generates a profit from its operations, this profit 'belongs' to the shareholders. Profits generally increase the net amount of assets less liabilities and this will be balanced in the accounting equation by an increase in equity.

The Income Statement and Double Entry Bookkeeping

We must extend the principles of double-entry bookkeeping introduced in the last chapter to cover transactions relating to the income statement.

We saw that the income statement analyses changes in equity. We already know that changes in equity are recorded according to the following table.

Table 4.6

	Debit	**Credit**
Increase in	An asset	A liability or equity item
Decrease in	A liability or equity item	An asset

Instead of debiting or crediting equity directly we now debit or credit accounts that refer to the income statement and then work out the cumulative effect on equity. For example when we sold the Muffins for €1,000 we know that this will increase the bank account and increase equity. We will debit bank and rather than credit equity directly we will credit a new account called revenue.

Table 4.7

	Debit	**Credit**
Increase in	An asset	A liability or equity item
Increase in	An expense or a loss	A revenue or a gain

Example 1

Take the T accounts of Murphy's Muffins as we left them at the end of the last chapter and record paying for €500 of ingredients and selling Muffins for €1,000. Here are the T accounts as we left them.

Table 4.8

Debit — **Bank** — **Credit**

Date	*Account*	*Amount*	*Date*	*Account*	*Amount*
...	Issued share capital	1,000	...	Machine	500
...	Bank Loan	1,500			

Debit — **Machine** — **Credit**

Date	*Account*	*Amount*	*Date*	*Account*	*Amount*
...	Bank	500			

Debit — **Bank Loan** — **Credit**

Date	*Account*	*Amount*	*Date*	*Account*	*Amount*
			...	Bank	1,500

Debit — **Issued Share Capital** — **Credit**

Date	*Account*	*Amount*	*Date*	*Account*	*Amount*
			...	Bank	1,000

In order to record the acquisition and payment for the ingredients we construct a journal entry. The ingredients cost €500 and were paid for immediately. Therefore, the bank account has decreased by €500 and we will credit the bank. We set up an account called 'Ingredient costs' and this will be debited with €500. The finished journal is:

Table 4.9 Journal entry to record sale of muffins

Date	**Account**	**Debit**	**Credit**
...	Ingredient costs (Income Statement)	500	
...	Bank		500

Being acquisition of ingredients for cash

Table 4.10

Debit		Bank			Credit
Date	*Account*	*Amount*	*Date*	*Account*	*Amount*
...	Issued share capital	1,000	...	Machine	500
...	Bank Loan	1,500	...	Ingredient costs	500

Debit		Ingredient Costs			Credit
Date	*Account*	*Amount*	*Date*	*Account*	*Amount*
...	Bank	500			

In order to record the sale of the Muffins for €1,000 cash we also construct a journal entry. The bank has increased by €1,000 so it will be debited. We open a new account called 'Revenue' and credit that account.

Table 4.11

Date	Account	Debit	Credit
...	Bank	1,000	
...	Revenue		1,000
Being sale of muffins			

Table 4.12

Debit		Bank			Credit
Date	*Account*	*Amount*	*Date*	*Account*	*Amount*
...	Issued share capital	1,000	...	Machine	500
...	Bank Loan	1,500	...	Ingredient costs	500
...	Revenue	1,000			

Debit		Ingredient Costs			Credit
Date	*Account*	*Amount*	*Date*	*Account*	*Amount*
...	Bank	500			

Debit		Revenue			Credit
Date	*Account*	*Amount*	*Date*	*Account*	*Amount*
			...	Bank	1,000

We now balance off all the T Accounts in Table 4.13.

Table 4.13

Debit — **Bank** — **Credit**

Date	*Account*	*Amount*	*Date*	*Account*	*Amount*
...	Issued share capital	1,000	...	Machine	500
...	Bank Loan	1,500	...	Ingredient costs	500
...	Revenue	1,000		Balance	2,500
		3,500			3,500
	Balance	2,500			

Debit — **Ingredient Costs** — **Credit**

Date	*Account*	*Amount*	*Date*	*Account*	*Amount*
...	Bank	500		Balance	500
		500			500
	Balance	500			

Debit — **Revenue** — **Credit**

Date	*Account*	*Amount*	*Date*	*Account*	*Amount*
	Balance	1,000	...	Bank	1,000
		1,000			1,000
				Balance	1,000

Debit — **Machine** — **Credit**

Date	*Account*	*Amount*	*Date*	*Account*	*Amount*
...	Bank	500		Balance	500
		500			500
	Balance	500			

Debit — **Bank Loan** — **Credit**

Date	*Account*	*Amount*	*Date*	*Account*	*Amount*
	Balance	1,500	...	Bank	1,500
		1,500			1,500
				Balance	1,500

Debit — **Issued Share Capital** — **Credit**

Date	*Account*	*Amount*	*Date*	*Account*	*Amount*
	Balance	1,000	...	Bank	1,000
		1,000			1,000
				Balance	1,000

The Trial balance is given in Table 4.14.

Table 4.14
Trial Balance for Murphy's Muffins as at 28 February, Year 1

Account	*Debit*	*Credit*
Bank	2,500	
Ingredient cost	500	
Revenue		1,000
Machine	500	
Bank loan		1,500
Issued share capital		1,000
	3,500	3,500

This trial balance shows the revenue account on the credit side and the ingredient cost account on the debit side. This is because increases in revenues are credits and increases in costs are debits. In a typical trial balance there will be many accounts that refer to the income statement rather than the statement of financial position.

Summary

When a business makes a profit it increases its net assets on the statement of financial position. This increase in net assets must be reflected in an increase in equity on the other side of the accounting equation. This increase in equity is analysed using the income statement. All of the entries involving revenues, gains, losses and expenses are posted to accounts that are summed in the income statement and then added to the retained income balance on the statement of financial position.

Chapter 4 Exercises

Exercise 4.1

Beancounter Ltd. started to trade in January. The transactions are given below:

Transaction Number	Date	Description
4	3 Jan	Beancounter Ltd. buys in widgets for €500 in cash.
5	4 Jan	Beancounter Ltd. sells all of the widgets for €1,000 in cash.
6	5 Jan	Beancounter Ltd. pays wages to Ms. Beancounter of €200 in cash.

(a) Prepare the statement of financial position of Beancounter Ltd. as at the 5th of January. Use the following table to trace through the transactions.

Statement of financial position as at 5 January

	Opening balance	**Tx. 4**	**Tx. 5**	**Tx. 6**	
Assets					
Van	1,000 dr				
Bank	500 dr	500 cr	1000 dr	200 cr	
=					1800
Equity					
Issued share capital Shares of €1.00 each	1,000 cr				
Retained income					300
+ Liabilities					
Bank loan	500 cr				
					1000

Income Statement for the period 1 January – 5 January

	Tx. 4	**Tx. 5**	**Tx. 6**	
Revenue		1000		
Purchases	500			
Wages			200	
Profit				300

(b) Prepare journal entries for each of the transactions

Tx. 4

Date	**Account**	**Debit**	**Credit**

Being

Tx. 5

Date	**Account**	**Debit**	**Credit**

Being

Tx. 6

Date	**Account**	**Debit**	**Credit**

Being

(c) Post each of the journal entries to T accounts using the template below. Balance each T account.

Debit		**Bank**			**Credit**
Date	*Account*	*Amount*	*Date*	*Account*	*Amount*
2.1	Balance	500			

Debit		**Van**			**Credit**
Date	*Account*	*Amount*	*Date*	*Account*	*Amount*
2.1	Balance	1,000			

Debit		**Bank Loan**			**Credit**
Date	*Account*	*Amount*	*Date*	*Account*	*Amount*
			2.1	Balance	500

Debit		**Issued Share Capital**			**Credit**
Date	*Account*	*Amount*	*Date*	*Account*	*Amount*
			2.1	Balance	1,000

Debit		**Purchases**			**Credit**
Date	*Account*	*Amount*	*Date*	*Account*	*Amount*

Debit		**Sales**			**Credit**
Date	*Account*	*Amount*	*Date*	*Account*	*Amount*

Debit		**Wages**			**Credit**
Date	*Account*	*Amount*	*Date*	*Account*	*Amount*

(d) Extract a trial balance from the T accounts

Trial Balance

Account	**Debit**	**Credit**
Bank		
Van		
Purchases		
Sales		
Wages		
Bank loan		
Issued share capital		

Chapter 5

Preparing Financial Statements – Part I

Introduction

We have covered the statement of financial position, the income statement and the fundamentals of the accounting system. It is now time to put these components together and to prepare a set of financial statements for a very straightforward business. This business is simple in that it will buy and sell everything for cash and will not deal on credit terms.

The Transactions

The transactions that this business enters into for the month of January are as follows.

Table 5.1
Transactions for Cupcake Ltd. in January

Transaction Number	Date	Description
1	1 Jan	Cupcake Ltd. is formed as a limited company and Mr. Byrne invests €10,000 for 10,000 shares of €1 each
2	1 Jan	Cupcake Ltd. receives a loan of €5,000 from the Bank of Dublin. This amount is received immediately into Cupcake Ltd.'s bank account.
3	2 Jan	Cupcake Ltd. hires a machine. The rental is €1,000 for one month's rent. This amount is paid immediately to the hire company.
4	2 Jan	Cupcake Ltd. rents premises. The rent is €5,000 for one month's rent. This amount is paid immediately to the landlord.
5	3 Jan	Cupcake Ltd. buys materials to make cupcakes for €8,000. This amount is paid immediately to the suppliers. All of these materials are used up during the month.

Table 5.1
Transactions for Cupcake Ltd. in January (continued)

6	3 Jan - 30 Jan	Cupcake Ltd. sells all of its cupcake output for the month to its customers. The customers pay €20,000 for all of the month's output.
7	30 Jan	The bank charges interest of €25 and deducts this from Cupcake's account.

The Transactions

This list of transactions is so simple we can immediately see what the financial statements will look like at the end of January. The income statement will show revenues of €20,000 and costs of ingredients (€8,000), rental of premises (€5,000), rental of machine (€1,000) and interest (€25). The income statement is show in Table 5.2.

Table 5.2 Cupcake Ltd. Income Statement for the period ended:

	31 January
Revenue (from trans. 6)	20,000
Less expenses	
Ingredients	(8,000)
Machine hire	(1,000)
Rent	(5,000)
Interest	(25)
Profit for the financial period	5,975

The main asset on the statement of financial position will be the bank account which could be derived as follows:

Table 5.3
Cupcake Ltd. - Calculation of the Bank balance at the end of January

Date	**Description**	**Amount €**
1. Jan	Opening bank account Bank balance	0
1 Jan	Capital contributed	+10,000
1 Jan	Receipt of loan	+5,000
2 Jan	Rent of machine	-1,000
2 Jan	Rent of premises	-5,000
3 Jan	Purchase of materials	-8,000
3 Jan – 30 Jan	Sales of cupcakes	+20,000
30 Jan	Interest	-25
31 Jan	Bank balance	20,975

This calculation allows us to prepare the statement of financial position:

Table 5.4 Cupcake Ltd. Statement of financial position as at:

	31 January
Assets	
Bank	20,975
Liabilities	
Bank loan	(5,000)
	15,975
Equity	
Issued share capital	10,000
Retained income	5,975
	15,975

Double Entry Bookkeeping for Cupcake Ltd.

In order to record Cupcake's transactions each event must be turned into a journal entry and then entered into Cupcake's T accounts. The first transaction is the issue of share capital. This will increase the bank by €10,000. Bank will be debited because it is an asset and it is increasing (See Table 4.5). In the equity section of the statement of financial position the equity share capital will increase by €10,000. Equity share capital will be credit as it is an equity item and it is increasing.

Table 5.5 Journal entry to record issue of share capital

Date	**Account**	**Debit**	**Credit**
1 Jan	Bank	10,000	
1 Jan	Equity share capital		10,000
Being issue of share capital			

The next transaction is the receipt of a loan of €5,000. This involves increasing the bank (debit) and creating a liability for the amount of the loan (credit)

Table 5.6 Journal entry to record receipt of loan

Date	**Account**	**Debit**	**Credit**
1 Jan	Bank	5,000	
1 Jan	Loan		5,000
Being receipt of loan			

Transaction 3 is the payment of rent of €1,000 on a machine. This rent will cover one month's use of the machine. This payment will decrease our bank account by €1,000 (credit). It is also an expense item in the income statement. We reflect this by debiting the machine rental account.

Table 5.7 Journal entry to record payment of rental on machine

Date	Account	Debit	Credit
2 Jan	Machine rental (Income Statement)	1,000	
2 Jan	Bank (Statement of financial position)		1,000
Being payment of rental on machine			

Transaction 4 is similar to transaction 3.

Table 5.8 Journal entry to record payment of rental on premises

Date	Account	Debit	Credit
2 Jan	Premises rental (Income Statement)	5,000	
2 Jan	Bank (Statement of financial position)		5,000
Being payment of rental on premises			

Transaction 5 is the purchase of materials. This decreases the bank account by €8,000 (credit). The other side of the entry is to the ingredients account. This is an income statement account. It is debited as it is an increase in costs.

Table 5.9 Journal entry to record purchase of materials

Date	Account	Debit	Credit
3 Jan	Ingredients (Income Statement)	8,000	
3 Jan	Bank (Statement of financial position)		8,000
Being purchase of materials			

Transaction 6 concerns the sales made to Cupcakes customers. The customers pay €20,000 for the month's output. This increases the bank account by €20,000 (debit). The other side of this entry is to revenue which is an income statement account.

Table 5.10 Journal entry to record revenue

Date	Account	Debit	Credit
30 Jan	Bank	20,000	
30 Jan	Revenue		20,000
Being revenue for January			

Transaction 7 concerns the interest charged on Cupcake's bank loan. The bank has charged €25 of interest for January which has been deducted from Cupcake's bank account. This means that the bank balance has decreased and should be credited. The other side of the entry is to record the interest as an expense by debiting the interest expense account.

Table 5.11 Journal entry to interest

Date	Account	Debit	Credit
30 Jan	Interest expense (income statement)	25	
30 Jan	Bank (statement of financial position)		25
Being interest for January			

These journals can now be posted to T accounts in order to work out the cumulative effect of the transactions for the month.

Table 5.11

Debit — **Bank (SOFP)** — **Credit**

Date	*Account*	*Amount*	*Date*	*Account*	*Amount*
1 Jan	Issued share capital	10,000	2 Jan	Machine rent	1,000
1 Jan	Bank loan	5,000	2 Jan	Premises rent	5,000
30 Jan	Revenue	20,000	3 Jan	Ingredient costs	8,000
			30 Jan	Interest	25
			31 Jan	Balance	20,975
		35,000			35,000
31 Jan	Balance	20,975			

Debit — **Ingredient Costs (IS)** — **Credit**

Date	*Account*	*Amount*	*Date*	*Account*	*Amount*
3 Jan	Bank	8,000	31 Jan	Balance	8,000
		8,000			8,000
31 Jan	Balance	8,000			

Table 5.11 (continued)

Revenue (IS[20])

Debit					Credit
Date	*Account*	*Amount*	*Date*	*Account*	*Amount*
31 Jan	Balance	20,000	30 Jan	Bank	20,000
		20,000			20,000
			31 Jan	Balance	20,000

Machine Rental (IS)

Debit					Credit
Date	*Account*	*Amount*	*Date*	*Account*	*Amount*
2 Jan	Bank	1,000	31 Jan	Balance	1,000
		1,000			1,000
31 Jan	Balance	1,000			

Premises Rental (IS)

Debit					Credit
Date	*Account*	*Amount*	*Date*	*Account*	*Amount*
2 Jan	Bank	5,000	31 Jan	Balance	5,000
		5,000			5,000
31 Jan	Balance	5,000			

Interest Expense (IS)

Debit					Credit
Date	*Account*	*Amount*	*Date*	*Account*	*Amount*
30 Jan	Bank	25	31 Jan	Balance	25
		25			25
31 Jan	Balance	25			

Bank Loan (SOFP)

Debit					Credit
Date	*Account*	*Amount*	*Date*	*Account*	*Amount*
31 Jan	Balance	5,000	1 Jan	Bank	5,000
		5,000			5,000
			31 Jan	Balance	5,000

[20] IS signifies an income statement account and SOFP signifies a statement of financial position account.

Table 5.11 (continued)

Debit		**Issued Share Capital (SOFP)**			**Credit**
Date	*Account*	*Amount*	*Date*	*Account*	*Amount*
31 Jan	Balance	10,000	1 Jan	Bank	10,000
		10,000			10,000
			31 Jan	Balance	10,000

Using the balances on the T accounts we can extract a trial balance (Table 5.12).

Table 5.12
Trial Balance for Cupcake Ltd. as at 31st January

Account	***Debit***	***Credit***
Bank	20,975	
Ingredient cost	8,000	
Revenue		20,000
Machine rental	1,000	
Premises rental	5,000	
Interest expense	25	
Bank loan		5,000
Issued share capital		10,000
	35,000	35,000

Preparing the Financial Statements from the Trial Balance

The trial balance gives us all of the information necessary to prepare financial statements. The first step is to classify each item as to whether it belongs in the Income Statement (IS) or the Statement of financial position (SOFP). Items can be identified by their descriptions and whether they have a debit or credit balance.

Table 5.13
Trial Balance for Cupcake Ltd. as at 31st January

Account	***Debit***	***Credit***	
Bank	20,975		SOFP
Ingredient cost	8,000		IS
Revenue		20,000	IS
Machine rental	1,000		IS
Premises rental	5,000		IS
Interest expense		25	IS
Bank loan		5,000	SOFP
Issued share capital		10,000	SOFP
	35,000	35,000	

Taking each of the items in the trial balance and slotting it into the correct place in the financial statements gives:

Table 5.14 Cupcake Ltd. Income Statement for the period ended:

	31 January
Revenue	20,000
Less expenses	
Ingredients	(8,000)
Machine rental	(1,000)
Premises Rent	(5,000)
Interest expense	(25)
Profit for the financial period	5,975

Table 5.15 Cupcake Ltd. Statement of financial position as at:

	31 January
Assets	
Bank	20,975
Liabilities	
Bank loan	(5,000)
	15,975
Equity	
Issued share capital	10,000
Retained income	5,975
	15,975

Summary

In this chapter we take a list of transactions and produce an income statement and a statement of financial position. In this case the transactions were so simple that the income statement could be produced directly and only the bank balance in the statement of financial position needed to be calculated. Alternatively, we can write down a journal entry for each of the transactions. This provides a recipe to record the transaction in T accounts. The T accounts can then be balanced and a trial balance can be prepared. This trial balance provided the basic information that is required to produce an income statement and a statement of financial position.

Chapter 5 Exercises

Exercise 5.1

Columbus Ltd. is formed by Mr. Johnson on 1 January. Its first 6 transactions are as follows:

Transaction Number	Date	Description
1	1 Jan	Columbus Ltd. is formed as a limited company and Mr. Johnson invests €30,000 for 30,000 shares of €1 each
2	1 Jan	Columbus Ltd. receives a loan of €20,000 from the Bank of Dublin. This amount is received immediately into Columbus Ltd.'s bank account.
3	2 Jan	Columbus Ltd. hires a motor vehicle. The rental is €700 for one month's rent. This amount is paid immediately to the hire company.
4	2 Jan	Columbus Ltd. rents premises. The rent is €2,500 for one month's rent. This amount is paid immediately to the landlord.
5	3 Jan	Columbus Ltd. buys materials to make products for €10,000. This amount is paid immediately to the suppliers. All of these materials are used up during the month.
6	3 Jan - 30 Jan	Columbus Ltd. sells all of its output for the month to its customers. The customers pay €25,000 for all of the month's output.
7	30 Jan	Bank of Dublin Charges Columbus Ltd. €120 interest. It is deducted directly from the bank account.

(a) Prepare the income statement and statement of financial position of Columbus Ltd. using the list of transactions above.

Columbus Ltd. Income Statement for the period ended:

	31 January
Revenue	
Less expenses	
Materials cost	
Motor vehicle hire	
Rent	
Interest expense	
Profit for the financial period	

Columbus Ltd. - Calculation of the Bank balance at the end of January

Date	Description	Amount €
1. Jan	Opening bank account Bank balance	0
31 Jan	Bank balance	

Columbus Ltd. Statement of financial position as at:

	31 January
Assets	
Bank	
Liabilities	
Bank loan	
Equity	
Issued share capital	
Retained income	

(b) Prepare journal entries for each of the transactions

Tx. 1

Date	Account	Debit	Credit

Being

Tx. 2

Date	Account	Debit	Credit

Being

Tx. 3

Date	Account	Debit	Credit

Being

Tx. 4

Date	Account	Debit	Credit

Being

Tx. 5

Date	Account	Debit	Credit

Being

Tx. 6

Date	Account	Debit	Credit

Being

Tx. 7

Date	Account	Debit	Credit

Being

(c) Record each of the transactions in T accounts.

Debit		**Bank (SOFP)**			**Credit**
Date	*Account*	*Amount*	*Date*	*Account*	*Amount*

Debit		**Materials Costs (IS)**			**Credit**
Date	*Account*	*Amount*	*Date*	*Account*	*Amount*

Debit		**Revenue (IS)**			**Credit**
Date	*Account*	*Amount*	*Date*	*Account*	*Amount*

Debit		**Motor Van Rental (IS)**			**Credit**
Date	*Account*	*Amount*	*Date*	*Account*	*Amount*

Debit		**Premises Rental (IS)**			**Credit**
Date	*Account*	*Amount*	*Date*	*Account*	*Amount*

Debit		**Interest Expense (IS)**			**Credit**
Date	*Account*	*Amount*	*Date*	*Account*	*Amount*

Debit		Bank Loan (SOFP)			Credit
Date	*Account*	*Amount*	*Date*	*Account*	*Amount*

Debit		Issued Share Capital (SOFP)			Credit
Date	*Account*	*Amount*	*Date*	*Account*	*Amount*

(d) Prepare a trial balance

Trial Balance for Columbus Ltd. as at 31st January

Account	***Debit***	***Credit***
Bank		
Materials cost		
Revenue		
Motor vehicle rental		
Premises rental		
Interest expense		
Bank loan		
Issued share capital		

Chapter 6

Revenues, Expenses and the Accruals Principle

Introduction

The Income Statement is based on the accruals principal. The accruals basis of accounting is described as follows by the IASB:

Figure 6.1
Extract from IASB Framework for the Preparation and Presentation of Financial Statements [21]

In order to meet their objectives, financial statements are prepared on the accrual basis of accounting. Under this basis, the effects of transactions and other events are recognised when they *occur* (and not as cash or its equivalent is received or paid) and they are recorded in the accounting records and reported in the financial statements of the periods to which they relate. (emphasis added)

The accruals basis of accounting means that transactions are recorded in the accounting reports when they occur. This contrasts with recording transactions when they are received or paid. For example, if a business sells goods on credit, the transaction occurs when the goods are shipped to the customer. The customer will pay the cost of the goods to the business at a later point. The accounting system recognises the sale when it occurs not when the customer pays for the goods. This means that the revenue figure in the income statement contains all the sales that occurred during the period. This is not necessarily the amount of money received from customers during the period.

Revenue Recognition

The firm's revenue recognition policy determines when the firm recognises a sale. Accounting has always distinguished between the making of a sale and the collection of the debt for that sale. Traditionally, firms recognized a sale when the goods were delivered to the customer. Applying this simple rule has become much more difficult as companies have used more complex sales

[21] IASC, 1989, "International Financial Reporting Standards - Framework for the Preparation and Presentation of Financial Statements" Para. 22

contracts. For example, software licences, goods on sale or return and customer subscriptions all constitute difficulties.

The International Accounting Standard which deals with revenue recognition takes a principles based approach. In essence, it insists that all of the risk and rewards of the goods or services should have passed to the customer and that the outcome of the transaction can be reliably measured before a sale can be recognised.

Figure 6.2
Extract from IAS 16 Revenue (Para. 14)

Revenue from the sale of goods shall be recognised when all the following conditions have been satisfied:

(a) The entity has transferred to the buyer the significant risks and rewards of ownership of the goods;
(b) the entity retains neither continuing managerial involvement to the degree usually associated with ownership nor effective control over the goods sold;
(c) the amount of revenue can be measured reliably;
(d) it is probable that the economic benefits associated with the transaction will flow to the entity; and
(e) the costs incurred or to be incurred in respect of the transaction can be measured reliably.

IAS 16 requires that the risks and rewards of ownership of the goods have passed to the buyer. For example, if the goods were damaged or destroyed the buyer would have to bear this loss. Goods are sometimes sold on 'sale or return.' This means that the buyer can return them to the seller without penalty. This kind of transaction would not normally qualify as a sale under IAS 16 until the buyer had indicated that they intended to keep the goods.

IAS 16 also requires that it is probable that that the revenue will be received by the business. If sales are made to customer with poor credit records or it becomes apparent that customers are not going to pay for goods that these sales cannot be recorded as revenue.

Some firms have simple revenue recognition policies. Most firms with a physical product recognise a sale when the product is delivered. For example the revenue recognition policy for CRH plc, an Irish building materials company, is presented in Figure 6.3. It is a model of clarity and brevity. This is because the company sells mainly manufactured products and the revenue recognition procedures for this business are well established and easy to understand.

Figure 6.3
CRH plc
Extract from Notes to Financial Statements
Annual Report 31 December 2005

Revenue recognition
Revenue represents the value of goods and services supplied to external customers and excludes intercompany sales, trade discounts and value added tax/sales tax.

In general, revenue is recognised to the extent that it is subject to reliable measurement, that it is probable that economic benefits will flow to the Group and that the significant risks and rewards of ownership have passed to the buyer. Revenue on long-term contracts is recognised in accordance with the percentage-of-completion method with the percentage-of-completion being computed on an input cost basis. No revenue is recognised if there is uncertainty regarding recovery of the consideration due at the outset of the transaction, associated costs or the possible return of goods.

High-tech firms may have a number of criteria that have to be met before a sale can be recognised. This complexity may indicate a much greater level of uncertainty about revenues than in more traditional situations. For example, the revenue recognition policy from Amazon.com, Inc.'s financial statements is reproduced in Figure 6.4. This policy deals with a number of complex and controversial issues. It starts by outlining the tests that Amazon.com uses to recognise revenue. It then deals with the revenue recognition implications of selling goods as an agent, discounts and promotional pricing, incentive offers, commissions and shipping. This is, of course, nothing wrong with this policy. Indeed, it is commendable that the policy is so detailed. However, the length and complexity of the policy indicates that managers must exercise careful judgement in recognising revenue. This means that the financial information produced by the company is subject to complex judgements that may make the resulting financial statements difficult to understand.

Figure 6.4
Amazon.com revenue recognition note

Revenue Recognition

We recognize revenue from product sales or services rendered when the following four revenue recognition criteria are met: persuasive evidence of an arrangement exists, delivery has occurred or services have been rendered, the selling price is fixed or determinable, and collectibility is reasonably assured. Additionally, revenue arrangements with multiple deliverables are divided into separate units of accounting if the deliverables in the arrangement meet the following criteria: the delivered item has value to the customer on a standalone basis; there is objective and reliable evidence of the fair value of undelivered items; and delivery of any undelivered item is probable.

We evaluate the criteria of Emerging Issues Task Force ("EITF") Issue No. 99-19, *Reporting Revenue Gross as a Principal Versus Net as an Agent*, in determining whether it is appropriate to record the gross amount of product sales and related costs or the net amount earned as commissions. Generally, when we are the primary party obligated in a transaction, are subject to inventory risk, have latitude in establishing prices and selecting suppliers, or have several but not all of these indicators, revenue is recorded gross. If we are not primarily obligated and amounts earned are determined using a fixed percentage, a fixed-payment schedule, or a combination of the two, we generally record the net amounts as commissions earned. Under our Syndicated Stores arrangements, we record gross product sales and costs since we own the inventory, set prices, and are responsible for fulfillment and customer service, and the other business earns a sales commission.

Product sales and shipping revenues, net of promotional discounts, rebates, and return allowances, are recorded when the products are shipped and title passes to customers. Retail items sold to customers are made pursuant to a sales contract that provides for transfer of both title and risk of loss upon our delivery to the carrier. Return allowances, which reduce product revenue by our best estimate of expected product returns, are estimated using historical experience. Amounts paid in advance for subscription services, including amounts received for online DVD rentals and other membership programs, are deferred and recognized as revenue over the subscription term.

Figure 6.4
Amazon.com revenue recognition note (cont.)

We periodically provide incentive offers to our customers to encourage purchases. Such offers include current discount offers, such as percentage discounts off current purchases, inducement offers, such as offers for future discounts subject to a minimum current purchase, and other similar offers. Current discount offers, when accepted by our customers, are treated as a reduction to the purchase price of the related transaction, while inducement offers, when accepted by our customers, are treated as a reduction to purchase price based on estimated future redemption rates. Redemption rates are estimated using our historical experience for similar inducement offers. Current discount offers and inducement offers are presented as a net amount in "Net sales."

Commissions and per-unit fees received from third-party sellers and similar amounts earned through our Merchant.com program are recognized when the item is sold by the third-party seller and our collectibility is reasonably assured. We record an allowance for estimated refunds on such commissions using historical experience.

Outbound shipping charges to customers are included in "Net sales" and, excluding amounts earned from third-party sellers where we don't provide fulfillment services, amounted to $420 million, $372 million, and $365 million for 2004, 2003, and 2002.

The ultimate test of revenue recognition policies is the speed with which revenues turn into cash. If revenues are not turning into cash, then receivables on the statement of financial position will be growing.

The policies and judgements that a company uses to recognise revenue are critical to the financial statements. These policies and judgements must reflect the realities of a company's business. If there are question marks over whether revenue will be collected in cash then the company should wait until the situation is resolved to record revenue.

Accounting for Purchases and Sales

When the business makes a sale it transfers goods or services to a third part in exchange for immediate payment or a promise of payment at a later date.

Table 6.1 Scone Ltd. Statement of financial position as at 31 December:

	20x1
	€
Non-Current Assets	
Property, plant and equipment	5,000
Current Assets	
Inventory	3,000
Bank	5,500
	13,500
Equity	
Equity share capital	4,000
Retained Income	9,500
	13,500

Table 6.2 Scone Ltd. Income Statement for the year ended 31 December:

	20x1
	€
Revenue	20,000
Less cost of sales	(15,000)
Gross profit	5,000
Less expenses	
All expenses	(2,500)
Net profit	2,500

Scone Ltd.'s financial statements are given in Tables 6.1 and 6.2 above. Suppose that Scone Ltd. buys goods for €300 on credit and immediately sells them for €500 to a customer who will pay for them in 3 months time.

The financial statements would change in two ways because of the purchase. Firstly, we would owe €300 to one of our suppliers and this would be shown in the current liabilities section of the statement of financial position. Secondly, we would have €300 of extra expenses in the income statement. These expenses would be classified as 'Cost of sales' as the goods were sold immediately.

The financial statements would also change in two ways because of the sale. Firstly, €500 of extra revenue would be recognised in the Income Statement. Secondly, a receivable of €500 would be recognised in the statement of financial position. This asset represents the amount that is due from the customer for the goods supplied.

Table 6.3 Scone Ltd. statement of financial position as at 31 December

	20x1	Purchase	Sale	Transfer	After the Purchase and Sale
	€	€	€		€
Non-Current Assets					
Property, plant and equipment	5,000				5,000
Current Assets					
Inventory	3,000				3,000
Receivables			500 dr		500
Bank	5,500				5,500
	13,500				14,000
Equity					
Equity share capital	4,000				4,000
Retained income	9,500			200 cr	9,700
	13,500			^	13,700
Current liabilities					
Payables		300 cr			300
	13,500				14,000
Income Statement for the year ended 31 December	20x1				
	€				€
Revenue	20,000		500 cr		20,500
Less cost of sales	(15,000)	300 dr			(15,300)
Gross profit	5,000				5,200
Less expenses					
All expenses	(2,500)				(2,500)
Net profit	2,500			200 cr	2,700

The purchase involves increasing the payables liability (credit) and increasing the purchases expense in the income statement (debit)[22].

Table 6.4 Journal Entry to Record Purchase of Goods on Credit

Date	Account	Debit	Credit
...	Purchases	300	
...	Payables		300
Being purchase of goods on credit			

The sale involves increasing the receivables asset (debit) and increasing the revenues in the income statement (credit).

Table 6.5 Journal Entry to Record Sale of Goods on Credit

Date	Account	Debit	Credit
...	Receivables	500	
...	Revenue		500
Being sale of goods on credit			

These transactions are recorded in Scone Ltd.'s T accounts in Table 6.6 below:

Table 6.6

Debit		**Receivables**			**Credit**
Date	*Account*	*Amount*	*Date*	*Account*	*Amount*
...	Sales	500			

Debit		**Revenue**			**Credit**
Date	*Account*	*Amount*	*Date*	*Account*	*Amount*
			...	Receivables	500

Debit		**Payables**			**Credit**
Date	*Account*	*Amount*	*Date*	*Account*	*Amount*
				Purchases	300

Debit		**Purchases**			**Credit**
Date	*Account*	*Amount*	*Date*	*Account*	*Amount*
	Payables	300			

[22] Refer to Table 4.5 in Chapter 4 for an explanation of double entry in the income statement.

The accruals principle requires that transactions are recorded when they occur rather than when there is a movement of cash. This means that sales must be recorded when goods are delivered to customers even if the customers only pay for them at a later date. This means that sales on credit are recorded by crediting revenue in the income statement and debiting receivables in the statement of financial position. This creates an asset on the statement of financial position and revenue in the income statement. Purchases are recorded by debiting purchases in the income statement and crediting payables in the statement of financial position. This creates a liability in the statement of financial position and an expense in the income statement.

Accounting for Receipts and Payments

The accruals principle requires that transactions are recorded when they occur rather than when they are received or paid. For example, a sale will be recorded when a customer takes delivery of goods even if they don't pay for the goods until some time later. When the sale is made the business sets up an asset representing the debt owed by the customer. The sales transaction recorded in Table 6.3 involved increasing receivables by €500. When the customer pays off this debt this receivable will be extinguished and the cash balance will be increased. The entry to record the receipt of payment from the customer is as follows:

Table 6.7 Journal Entry to Record Receipt of Cash from a Customer

Date	Account	Debit	Credit
...	Bank	500	
...	Receivables		500

The receipt of the cash from the customer will be reflected in the statement of financial position. Table 6.8 shows how the statement of financial position changes when the customer pays their debt of €500.

Table 6.8

Scone Ltd. **Statement of financial position as at 31 December**	**20x1**	**Receipt of cash from a Customer**	**After the receipt**
	€	€	€
Non-Current Assets			
Property, plant and equipment	5,000		5,000
Current Assets			
Inventory	3,000		3,000
Receivables	500	500 cr	0
Bank	5,500	500 dr	6,000
	14,000		14,000
Equity			
Equity share capital	4,000		4,000
Retained income	9,700		9,700
	13,700		13,700
Current liabilities			
Payables	300		300
	14,000		14,000

Accounting for Expenses

Businesses have many types of expenses that must be included in the income statement. These include wages and salaries, distribution costs and administration expenses. The accruals principle requires that transactions are recorded when they occur and not when cash is received or paid. This means that expenses must be recorded when they occur. For example, if a business pays its rent quarterly in arrears not all of the rent payments may occur in the accounting period to which the rent relates. Table 6.9 shows the periods for which the rent is payable and the dates the rent is actually paid.

Table 6.9 Rent Payments

Rent period	**Date Rent paid**
1 Jan – 31 Mar	5 Apr
1 Apr – 30 Jun	7 Jul
1 Jul – 30 Sept	5 Oct
1 Oct – 31 Dec	8 Jan (of the following year)

The payment for the last quarter of the year (from 1 Oct – 31 Dec) is made on the 8th of January of the following year. If only rent paid during the accounting year was recorded then only three-quarters of the year's rent would have been shown as an expense during this year. The accruals principle requires that all of the rent that has been incurred in the financial year be shown as an expense in that year regardless of when it was paid.

Figure 6.5
Definitions of Accruals and Prepayments

An accrual occurs when expenses of one accounting period are paid in a later accounting period.

A prepayment occurs when expenses of an accounting period are paid in advance of that accounting period.

Accounting for Accruals

Scone Ltd. had rented premises on 1 January 20x1. On 31 December 20x1 (the date of its statement of financial position) it had not made any rent payments. The rent for the year was €1,000. In order to record this transaction a liability for the rent due must be created. This is called an accrual (see Figure 6.5). An expense for the rent incurred during the 20x1 accounting year must be shown in the income statement.

Table 6.10

Scone Ltd. Statement of financial position as at 31 December 20x1	**Before Rent expense**	**Rent Expense**	**Transfer to Retained Income**	**After Rent Expense**
	€	€		€
Non-Current Assets				
Property, plant and equipment	5,000			5,000
Current Assets				
Inventory	3,000			3,000
Receivables	500			500
Bank	5,500			5,500
	14,000			14,000
Equity				
Share capital	4,000			4,000
Retained Income	9,700		1,000 dr	8,700
	13,700		^	12,700
Current liabilities				
Payables	300			300
Accruals (Rent due)		1,000 cr		1,000
	14,000			14,000
Income Statement for the year ended 31 December				
	€			€
Revenue	20,500			20,500
Less cost of sales	(15,300)			(15,300)
Gross profit	5,200			5,200
Less expenses				
Rent expense		1,000 dr		(1,000)
All expenses	(2,500)			(2,500)
Net profit	2,700		1,000 dr	1,700

The double entry is to create a liability for the rent accrual (credit) and create an expense in the income statement for rent (debit).

Table 6.11 Journal Entry to Record Rent Accrual

Date	Account	Debit	Credit
...	Rent expense (Income statement)	1,000	
...	Rent Accrual (Statement of financial position)		1,000
Being rent accrual			

When the rent is paid in January of the following financial year the journal entry would be:

Table 6.12 Journal Entry to Record Rent Payment (in January of following year)

Date	Account	Debit	Credit
Jan x2	Rent Accrual (Statement of financial position)	1,000	
Jan x2	Bank		1,000
Being rent payment in January 20x2			

This would cancel out the credit balance on the rent accrual account and reduce the bank account.

Table 6.13

Scone Ltd. **Statement of financial position as at 31 December 20x1**	**At year end**	**Payment of Rent in January**	**After Rent Payment**
	€	€	€
Non-Current Assets			
Property, plant and equipment	5,000		5,000
Current Assets			
Inventory	3,000		3,000
Receivables	500		500
Bank	5,500	1,000 cr	4,500
	14,000		13,000
Equity			
Share capital	4,000		4,000
Retained Income	8,700		8,700
	12,700		12,700
Current liabilities			
Payables	300		300
Accruals (Rent due)	1,000	1000 dr	0
	14,000		13,000

Table 6.13 shows the effect of the rent payment in January. This payment has no effect on the income statement as the expense had been shown in the income statement already. The payment reduces the bank account and cancels out the liability for rent that is shown in the statement of financial position.

Accounting for Prepayments

Suppose that Scone Ltd. had paid insurance of €500 in December of 20x1. This insurance payment will provide cover from 1 July 20x1 to 30 June 20x2. This means that half of this payment relates to insurance services that will be received in the following accounting period (20x2).

We will first record the payment of the insurance.

Table 6.14 Scone Ltd. Statement of financial position as at 31 December 20x1	**Before Insurance payment**	**Insurance payment**		**After Insurance Payment**
	€	€		€
Non-Current Assets				
Property, plant and equipment	5,000			5,000
Current Assets				
Inventory	3,000			3,000
Receivables	500			500
Bank	5,500	500 cr		5,000
	14,000			13,500
Equity				
Share capital	4,000			4,000
Retained Income	8,700		500 dr	8,200
	12,700			12,200
Current liabilities				
Payables	300			300
Accruals (Rent due)	1,000			1,000
	14,000			13,500

Income Statement for the year ended 31 December				
	€			€
Revenue	20,500			20,500
Less cost of sales	(15,300)			(15,300)
Gross profit	5,200			5,200
Less expenses				
Rent expense	(1,000)			(1,000)
Insurance expense		500 dr		(500)
All expenses	(2,500)			(2,500)
Net profit	1,700		500 dr	1,200

The following journal records the payment of €500 of insurance. This involved reducing the bank by €500 (credit) and increasing the insurance expense (credit).

Table 6.15 Journal Entry to Record Insurance Payment

Date	Account	Debit	Credit
...	Insurance expense	500	
...	Bank		500
Being insurance payment			

An insurance expense of €500 has been recorded in the financial statements. However, only €250 of the insurance services has been used up. The remaining €250 will be used up in the next accounting period (20x2). We need to record a prepayment of €250 in order to reflect the fact that only €250 of expenses have been incurred in this accounting period and that we have an asset of €250 of insurance services.

Table 6.16

Scone Ltd. Statement of financial position as at 31 December 20x1	**Before Insurance payment**	**Insurance payment**		**After Insurance Payment**
	€	€		€
Non-Current Assets				
Property, plant and equipment	5,000			5,000
Current Assets				
Inventory	3,000			3,000
Receivables	500			500
Prepayment (insurance)		250 dr		250
Bank	5,000			5,000
	13,500			13,750
Equity				
Share capital	4,000			4,000
Retained Income	8,200		250cr	8,450
	12,200		^	12,450
Current liabilities				
Payables	300			300
Accruals (Rent due)	1,000			1,000
	13,500			13,750

Income Statement for the year ended 31 December				
	€			€
Revenue	20,500			20,500
Less cost of sales	(15,300)			(15,300)
Gross profit	5,200			5,200
Less expenses				
Rent expense	(1,000)			(1,000)
Insurance expense	(500)	250 cr		(250)
All expenses	(2,500)			(2,500)
Net profit	1,200		250cr	1,450

Setting up a prepayment involves reducing the expense in this year's income statement and recording an asset equal to the amount of the prepayment. This is achieved by debiting insurance prepayment to create an asset and crediting insurance expense to reduce the expense.

Table 6.17 Journal Entry to Record Insurance Prepayment

Date	Account	Debit	Credit
...	Insurance prepayment (Statement of financial position)	250	
...	Insurance expense (Income statement)		250
Being insurance prepayment			

The financial statements now show an insurance expense of €250 for the year which reflects the fact that even though €500 was paid for insurance only €250 of insurance services was used. The remaining €250 of insurance services is shown as a prepayment on the statement of financial position.

Summary

The accruals principle states that transactions should be included in the financial statements when they have occurred. This means that a sale should be recorded as revenue when the goods have been delivered to a customer rather than when that customer pays for the goods. Expenses should also be recorded when they occur. This means that if goods have been delivered or services have been consumed then these transactions must be recorded in the financial statements. It does not matter whether payment has been made for the goods or services. This requires the recording of accruals and prepayments in the statement of financial position and increasing or decreasing expenses in the income statement.

Chapter 6 Exercises

Exercise 6.1

When should each of the following transactions be recognised in the revenue figure in the financial statements?

- A plc signs a contract to sell a piece of land to B plc for €2m subject to planning permission for 20 houses on the land being granted. This permission will be decided at a meeting of the local council in one month's time.
- Garage plc sells a second hand car for €12,000. The car comes with a two year warranty.
- Fun plc sells €40,000 of video games to a retail store. The games are on a sale or return basis.
- Fly-by-nite plc, an airline, sells a ticket to fly from Dublin to Paris in 2 months time for €200.

Exercise 6.2

Danish Pastry Ltd.'s financial statements for the year ended 31 December 20x6 are presented below (left most column of Exhibit 1). The following transactions have not been recorded in the financial statements. Record these transactions using Exhibit 1. Prepare Journals for each transaction and record the transactions using the T accounts in Exhibit 3.

Transaction	*Details*
1	Goods were purchases on credit for €700.
2	Sales of €1,000 were made on credit.
3	Sales of €300 were made for cash. (This sale and the sale in Tx. 2 relate to the goods purchases in Tx.1 above. i.e. these transactions have no impact on inventory)
4	The company discovers that it owes wages of €300 to one of its employees.
5	The company accountant discovers an ESB bill under a pile of papers. It is for €200 and it's for the period ending 31/12/x6.
6	The company's insurance for the year was renewed on 1 July 20x6 for one year. The cost for one year's insurance was €500. This amount was fully paid and appears on the income statement as an expense.

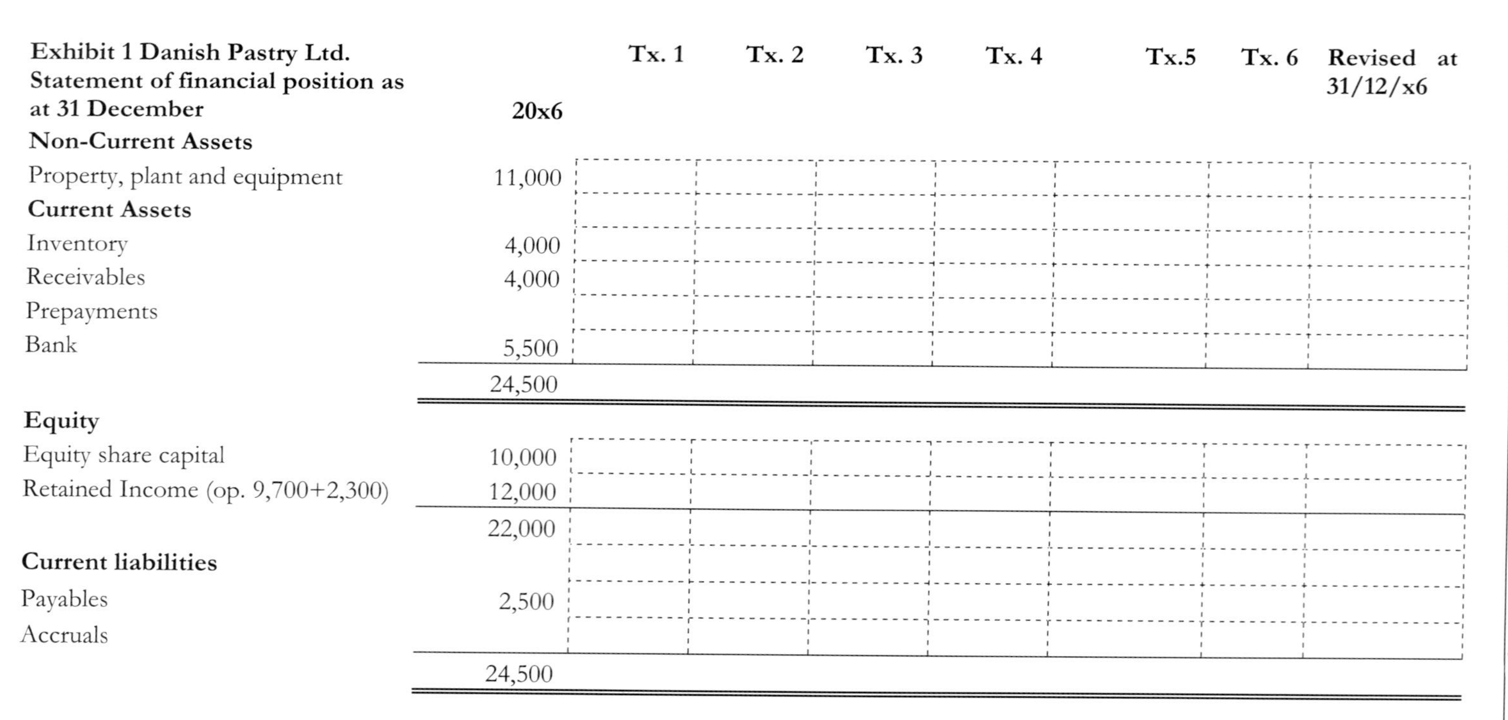

Exhibit 1 Danish Pastry Ltd. Statement of financial position as at 31 December	20x6	Tx. 1	Tx. 2	Tx. 3	Tx. 4	Tx.5	Tx. 6	Revised at 31/12/x6
Non-Current Assets								
Property, plant and equipment	11,000							
Current Assets								
Inventory	4,000							
Receivables	4,000							
Prepayments								
Bank	5,500							
	24,500							
Equity								
Equity share capital	10,000							
Retained Income (op. 9,700+2,300)	12,000							
	22,000							
Current liabilities								
Payables	2,500							
Accruals								
	24,500							

Income Statement for the year ended 31 December 20x6	**20x6**	**Tx. 1**	**Tx. 2**	**Tx. 3**	**Tx. 4**	**Tx.5**	**Tx. 6**	**Revised at 31/12/x6**
Revenue	100,000							
Less cost of sales	(75,000)							
Gross profit	25,000							
Wages	(3,000)							
Light & heat	(1,200)							
Insurance	(500)							
All other expenses	(18,000)							
Net profit	2,300							

Exhibit 2 Journal Entries

Tx. 1

Date	Account	Debit	Credit

Being

Tx. 2

Date	Account	Debit	Credit

Being

Tx. 3

Date	Account	Debit	Credit

Being

Tx. 4

Date	Account	Debit	Credit

Being

Tx. 5

Date	Account	Debit	Credit

Being

Tx. 6

Date	Account	Debit	Credit

Being

Exhibit 3 Danish Pastry Ltd.'s T Accounts

Debit — **Receivables (SOFP)** — **Credit**

Date	*Account*	*Amount*	*Date*	*Account*	*Amount*

Debit — **Prepayments (SOFP)** — **Credit**

Date	*Account*	*Amount*	*Date*	*Account*	*Amount*

Debit — **Bank (SOFP)** — **Credit**

Date	*Account*	*Amount*	*Date*	*Account*	*Amount*

Debit — **Payables (SOFP)** — **Credit**

Date	*Account*	*Amount*	*Date*	*Account*	*Amount*

Debit — **Accruals (SOFP)** — **Credit**

Date	*Account*	*Amount*	*Date*	*Account*	*Amount*

Debit **Revenue (IS)** **Credit**

Date	*Account*	*Amount*	*Date*	*Account*	*Amount*

Debit **Purchases (IS)** **Credit**

Date	*Account*	*Amount*	*Date*	*Account*	*Amount*

Debit **Wages (IS)** **Credit**

Date	*Account*	*Amount*	*Date*	*Account*	*Amount*

Debit **Light & Heat (IS)** **Credit**

Date	*Account*	*Amount*	*Date*	*Account*	*Amount*

Debit **Insurance (IS)** **Credit**

Date	*Account*	*Amount*	*Date*	*Account*	*Amount*

NOTE: This is an incomplete set of T Accounts. You are only provided with the accounts that are required to record transactions 1-6.

Chapter 7

Assets

Introduction

In Chapter 1, we saw that 'an ***asset*** is a resource controlled by the entity as a result of past events and from which future economic benefits are expected to flow to the entity.'

Control over Resources

The definition of an asset states that it is '... a resource controlled by the entity ...' Notice that the definition stresses control rather than legal ownership. Accounting rules emphasise this distinction in a number of areas. One of the most striking is in the area of leased assets. When companies lease assets they enter into an agreement to pay a certain amount of money each period to use the asset. The lessee (usually a bank or a leasing company) retains ownership of the asset. The accounting problem here arises from the similarity between long term leasing and owning the asset. If a machine is expected to last about 10 years and a company leases that machine for 10 years and pays the full price of the machine plus interest in leasing charges then this is a very similar transaction to borrowing the money from the bank and purchasing the machine. If leased assets were omitted from business's statement of financial position then the company who borrowed the money and purchased the asset would have a very different statement of financial position from the business who leased the asset.

Future Economic Benefits

The definition of an asset states that it is something ' ... from which future economic benefits are expected to flow to the entity.' If economic benefits are expected to flow in the short term (usually within one year) then the asset is classified as a 'Current' asset. If the benefits are expected to flow after one year then the asset is classified as a 'Non-Current Asset.'

The certainty with which economic benefits will flow from potential assets is a major concern in deciding whether an item should be recognised as an asset. Consider three different potential assets. Firstly, the businesses bank balance is an asset that can be turned into economic benefits very easily and quickly.

Secondly, the businesses buildings will provide accommodation benefits for the company for many years to come. These buildings are usually considered assets because it is reasonable certain that they will provide economic benefits to the business. Thirdly, consider a businesses investment in Research and Development (R&D). This investment may be very important for the future prosperity of the business but the benefits from this investment may be uncertain at the time the investment is made. A pharmaceutical company could invest €200 million in the search for a cure for a particular type of disease. This investment could lead to a new drug for that disease, it could lead to better understanding of the disease but no new products or it could lead to a dead end with no advances what so ever. Obviously, the pharmaceutical company is optimistic about the investment but it cannot be certain about the future benefits in the same way as if it had invested in a new building. Table 7.1 gives some common assets and the benefits that can be expected from them.

Table 7.1

Type of asset	**Expected future benefits**	**Certainty of benefits**
Cash/Bank balance	Can be converted quickly into any type of good or service	Certain
Receivable	Will be converted into cash reasonably quickly.	Reasonably certain. Risk of doubtful debts.
Inventory	Will be converted into cash reasonably quickly.	Reasonably certain. Risk of damage or obsolesce.
Land and buildings	Will provide accommodation for the businesses operations	Reasonably certain.
Research and development	Will provide new products, services or processes for the businesses in the future	Uncertain

Verifiability of Past Transactions

Even if the item meets the asset recognition tests of control and expected future benefits it may still not be recognised as an asset. The value of the asset must be established in a past transaction or event. Usually, this transaction is the acquisition of the asset in a market transaction with another party who is independent from the business. For example, many businesses sell their products and services under a brand name. It is widely recognised that brand names such as Intel, Coke and Gillette have significant value. These brand names enable these businesses to sell their products in greater quantities and at higher prices than non-branded products. However, the value of these brands is often omitted from the statement of financial position. This is because the brands have been developed within the company and have never been subject to a market transaction. Accountants argue that the value of the brands is reflected in the financial statements over time as they provided superior profits but that they cannot be directly recognised on the statement of financial position. However, if a business purchases a brand from another company then it may be possible to recognise the brand as an asset because it has been subject to a market transaction.

Current and Non-Current Assets

Assets are divided into current and non-current. Figure 7.1 gives the IFRS rules for the classification of assets. Short term items are classified as current and items that will remain as assets for longer periods are classified as non-current.

Figure 7.1
IFRS Definitions (IAS 1 para. 57)

An asset shall be classified as current when it satisfies any of the following criteria:

(a) it is expected to be realised in, or is intended for sale or consumption in, the entity's normal operating cycle;
(b) it is held primarily for the purpose of being traded;
(c) it is expected to be realised within twelve months after the statement of financial position date; or
(d) it is cash or a cash equivalent (as defined in IAS 7 Statement of Cash Flows) unless it is restricted from being exchanged or used to settle a liability for at least twelve months after the statement of financial position date.

All other assets shall be classified as non-current

Non-Current Assets and Depreciation

We have seen above that some assets provide economic benefits over long periods of time. For example, a machine could provide benefits for 5 to 10 years. IAS 16 defines property, plant and equipment as follows:

Figure 7.2
IFRS Definitions (IAS 16)

Property, plant and equipment are tangible items that:
(a) are held for use in the production or supply of goods or services, for rental to others, or for administrative purposes; and
(b) are expected to be used during more than one period.

Land, buildings, motor vehicles, machines, office equipment and fixtures and fittings are all examples of this category of non-current asset. These items are acquired in order to give economic benefits to the business over more than one year.

Obviously, as these assets get older the economic benefits that they can provide are used up. An accounting procedure called depreciation is used to reflect this. IAS 16 provides the following definitions:

Figure 7.3
IFRS Definitions (IAS 16)

Depreciation is the systematic allocation of the depreciable amount of an asset over its useful life.

Depreciable amount is the cost of an asset, or other amount substituted for cost, less its residual value.

Useful life is:
(a) the period over which an asset is expected to be available for use by an entity; or
(b) the number of production or similar units expected to be obtained from the asset by an entity.

The residual value of an asset is the estimated amount that an entity would currently obtain from disposal of the asset, after deducting the estimated costs of disposal, if the asset were already of the age and in the condition expected at the end of its useful life.

Let's look at these definitions using an example. A business buys a machine on the 1st of January for €20,000. This machine will be used for 12 years at which time it is expected that it could be sold for €2,000. At the end of the first year of the machine's life the business must reflect the fact that some of the economic benefits of owing the machine have been used up. IAS 16 tells us that the 'Depreciable amount' is the cost of the asset (€20,000) less any residual value. Residual value is what the business could get for the machine at the end of its life (€2,000).

Table 7.2 Calculation of Depreciable Amount

	31 December
Cost of machine	20,000
Less residual value	(2,000)
Depreciable amount	18,000

The useful life of the asset is the period over which an asset is expected to be available for use by an entity. In this case the business expects to use the asset over 12 years. According to the definition of depreciation the depreciable amount must be spread over the asset's useful life. The way in which this 'spreading' is done is called the depreciation method. IAS 16 states the following:

Figure 7.4
IFRS Definitions (IAS 16)

The depreciation method used shall reflect the pattern in which the asset's future economic benefits are expected to be consumed by the entity.

In this case we will assume that roughly the same economic benefits flow from the asset in each year of its useful life. This enables us to use the simplest depreciation method which is called the straight-line method of depreciation.

Figure 7.5
Straight-line method of depreciation

$$\text{Depreciation charge for the period} = \frac{\text{depreciable amount}}{\text{useful life}}$$

or

$$\text{Depreciation charge for the period} = \frac{\text{cost less residual value}}{\text{useful life}}$$

In this case the depreciation charge for the first year of the asset's life would be the depreciable amount (18,000) divided by the useful life (12 years) which equal €1,500.

Table 7.3 Calculation of One Year's Depreciation Charge (using the straight-line method)

	31 December
Depreciable amount	18,000
÷ useful life	12 years
Depreciation charge for one year	1,500

This depreciation charge reflects the estimate of the amount of economic benefits that have been used up because of using the machine for one year.

The Impact of Depreciation on the Income Statement and Statement of Financial Position

Depreciation has an effect on both the income statement and on the statement of financial position. The following example illustrates this dual effect.

Table 7.4 The Statement of Financial Position and Income Statement of Doughnut Ltd.

Statement of financial position as at 31 December	**31.12.X3**	**31.12.X2**	**31.12.X1**
	€	€	€
Non-Current Assets			
Machine A at cost	1,000	1,000	1,000
Machine B at cost	2,000	2,000	
Current Assets			
Bank	400	400	500
Other asset and liabilities	11,100	7,100	5,500
	14,500	10,500	7,000
Equity			
Equity share capital	4,000	4,000	4,000
Retained Income	10,500	6,500	3,000
	14,500	10,500	7,000

Table 7.4 (Cont.)

Income Statement for the year ended 31 December	**31.12.X3**	**31.12.X2**	**31.12.X1**
	€	€	€
Sales	22,000	21,000	20,000
Less cost of sales	(16,000)	(15,500)	(15,000)
Gross profit	6,000	5,500	5,000
Less expenses			
All expenses (excluding depreciation)	(2,000)	(2,000)	(2,000)
Net profit	4,000	3,500	3,000

The financial statements of Doughnut Ltd. show three years of information. The first year ended 31 December 20X1 is on the right most side of the table. On the 1st of January 20X1 Doughnut purchased a machine (Machine A) for €1,000. They estimate this machine will last 10 years and have to be scrapped at that point. On the 1st of January 20X2 Doughnut still had this machine and purchased a second machine (Machine B) for €2,000. This machine will also last 10 years.

The financial statements given above do not reflect any depreciation. The first task in incorporating depreciation into these financial statements is to work out the depreciation charge for the machines in each year. Doughnut uses the straight-line method of depreciation.

Table 7.5 Calculation of Depreciation for Machine A for 20X1

	31 December
Depreciable amount	1,000
÷ useful life	10 years
Depreciation charge for one year	100

This calculation means that Doughnut Ltd. used up €100 of the economic benefits of Machine A using 20X1. This will be reflected in the financial statements by doing two things. Firstly, we will reduce the book value of the asset on the statement of financial position. Secondly, we will show the use of economic benefits as an expense in the income statement.

Table 7.6

Statement of Financial Position as at 31 December	**31.12.X1**
	€
Non-Current Assets	
Machine A at cost	1,000
Less accumulated depreciation	(100)
Net book value of Machine A	900
Current Assets	
Bank	500
Other asset and liabilities	5,500
	6,900
Equity	
Equity share capital	4,000
Retained Income	2,900
	6,900

Income Statement for the year ended 31 December	**31.12.X1**
	€
Sales	20,000
Less cost of sales	(15,000)
Gross profit	5,000
Less expenses	
All expenses (excluding depreciation)	(2,000)
Depreciation	(100)
Net profit	2,900

The depreciation charge is subtracted from the cost of Machine A on the statement of financial position. Rather than subtracting the figure directly, we allow depreciation to build up in an account called accumulated depreciation which is subtracted from the cost of Machine A. The cost of the asset less accumulated depreciation is know as the Net Book Value (NBV) of the asset. In this case the NBV is €900. In the income statement the depreciation charge is shown as an expense. This reduces the profit for X1 to €2,900 and this profit is carried through to retained income in the equity section of the statement of financial position. These changes can also be explained using the accounting equation:

Figure 7.6
The Accounting Equation

Assets – Liabilities = Equity
(100) (100)

In 19X2 Machine A must be depreciated again and Machine B must be depreciated for the first time.

Table 7.7 Calculation of Depreciation for Machine B for X2

	31 December
Depreciable amount	2,000
÷ useful life	10 years
Depreciation charge for one year	200

Table 7.8 shows the financial statements for the three years adjusted for depreciation.

Table 7.8

Statement of financial position as at 31 December	**31.12.X3**	**31.12.X2**	**31.12.X1**
	€	€	€
Non-Current Assets			
Machine A at cost	1,000	1,000	1,000
Less accumulated depreciation on A	(300)	(200)	(100)
Net book value of Machine A	700	800	900
Machine B at cost	2,000	2,000	
Less accumulated depreciation on B	(400)	(200)	
Net book value of Machine B	1,600	1,800	
Current Assets			
Bank	400	400	500
Other asset and liabilities	11,100	7,100	5,500
	13,800	10,100	6,900
Equity			
Equity share capital	4,000	4,000	4,000
Retained Income	9,800	6,100	2,900
	13,800	10,100	6,900

Income Statement for the year ended 31 December	**31.12.X3**	**31.12.X2**	**31.12.X1**
	€	€	€
Sales	22,000	21,000	20,000
Less cost of sales	(16,000)	(15,500)	(15,000)
Gross profit	6,000	5,500	5,000
Less expenses			
All expenses (excluding depreciation)	(2,000)	(2,000)	(2,000)
Depreciation on Machine A	(100)	(100)	(100)
Depreciation on Machine B	(200)	(200)	
Net profit	3,700	3,200	2,900

The adjusted financial statements show a number of differences from those in Table 7.4. Firstly, the depreciation charge for each asset in each year has been added to accumulated depreciation in the statement of financial position. These amounts are then subtracted from the cost of the asset to give the Net Book

Value of the asset. Secondly, the depreciation charge is show as an expense in the Income Statement. This reduces the net profit for the year and this feeds through to retained income in the statement of financial position. The effect of depreciation has been to reduce the assets of the business and also to reduce the equity of the business.

Recording Depreciation using Double-Entry Bookkeeping

Depreciation is recorded using two T accounts. The first is the accumulated depreciation T account. This account offsets the cost of the asset on the statement of financial position. The cost of the asset is a debit balance because it is an asset. Therefore in order to offset the cost of the asset we must credit the accumulated depreciation T account. The second T account used here is an Income Statement T account called 'Depreciation expense'. This T account will feed into the Income Statement in the same way as the rent or wages expense.

Table 7.9 Journal Entry to Record Depreciation on Machine A in 20X1

Date	**Account**	**Debit**	**Credit**
31/12/X1	Depreciation expense (Income Statement)	100	
31/12/X1	Accumulated depreciation		100

Being acquisition of ingredients for cash

This journal is recorded in the T accounts as follows:

Table 7.10

Debit		**Depreciation Expense (Income Statement)**			**Credit**
Date	*Account*	*Amount*	*Date*	*Account*	*Amount*
31/12/X1	Accumulated Depreciation	100			

Debit		**Accumulated Depreciation (Statement of financial position)**			**Credit**
Date	*Account*	*Amount*	*Date*	*Account*	*Amount*
			31/12/X1	Depreciation Expense	100

Recording the Acquisition of a Non-Current Asset

When a non-current asset is acquired by the business the new asset must be reflected in the statement of financial position and the reduction in the bank balance must also be recorded. When Doughnut Ltd. Acquired Machine A for €1,000 in cash it would have made the following entry.

Table 7.11 Journal Entry to Record Acquisition of Machine A

Date	Account	Debit	Credit
1/1/X1	Machine A	1,000	
1/1/X1	Bank		1,000
Being acquisition of Machine A for cash			

Table 7.12

Debit — **Machine A** — **Credit**

Date	*Account*	*Amount*	*Date*	*Account*	*Amount*
31/12/X1	Bank	1,000			

Debit — **Bank** — **Credit**

Date	*Account*	*Amount*	*Date*	*Account*	*Amount*
			31/12/X1	Machine A	1,000

Recording the Disposal of a Non-Current Asset

Recording the disposal of a non-current asset is more complex. The objective of the procedure is to remove the asset from the statement of financial position and replace it with either the cash or another asset that was received in exchange. The asset being disposed of can be shown on the statement of financial position at a value either greater or less than the cash or asset received in exchange. In this case the gain or loss made on the disposal of the asset must also be calculated and reflected in the Income Statement.

Suppose at the end of X3 Doughnut Ltd. sells Machine A for €400 in cash. The economic effect of this transaction is that Doughnut no longer has Machine A and has €400 in cash instead. In accounting terms, Machine A must be removed from the statement of financial position and €400 must be added to the bank balance. However, Machine A is valued at €700 on Doughnut's Statement of financial position. It cost €1,000 and €300 of depreciation has been charged against it. This means that Doughnut has made a loss on the disposal of the asset.

Table 7.13 Calculation of gain or loss on disposal of Machine A

	31 December
Cost of Machine A	1,000
Accumulated depreciation	(300)
Net Book Value	700
Proceeds from sale of Machine A	400
Loss on sale of asset	(300)

We will now adjust Doughnut's financial statements to reflect the disposal of Machine A on the last day of the X3 accounting period.

Table 7.14

Statement of financial position as at 31 December	**31.12.X3**	**Disposal**	**After Disposal**
	€	€	€
Non-Current Assets			
Machine A at cost	1,000	1,000 cr	0
Less accumulated depreciation on A	(300)	300 dr	0
Net book value of Machine A	700	700 cr	0
Machine B at cost	2,000		2,000
Less accumulated depreciation on B	(400)		(400)
Net book value of Machine B	1,600		1,600
Current Assets			
Bank	400	400 dr	800
Other asset and liabilities	11,100		11,100
	13,800		13,500
Equity			
Equity share capital	4,000		4,000
Retained Income	9,800		*9,500
	13,800		13,500

Table 7.14 (cont.)

Income Statement for the year ended 31 December	**31.12.X3**		**31.12.X3**
	€		€
Sales	22,000		22,000
Less cost of sales	(16,000)		(16,000)
Gross profit	6,000		6,000
Less expenses			
All expenses (excluding depreciation)	(2,000)		(2,000)
Depreciation on Machine A	(100)		(100)
Loss on disposal of Machine A		300 dr	(300)
Depreciation on Machine b	(200)		(200)
Net profit	3,700		3,400

* Note that retained income has decreased by €300 due to the decrease in the net profit in the income statement.

The effect of these changes has been (a) to remove Machine A from the statement of financial position, (b) to increase the bank by €400 and (c) to take the difference between the book value of the asset and what was received for it to the income statement.

The double entry for this transaction involves opening a special T called 'Disposal of Machine A.' The balance on this T account will be taken to the Income Statement and represents the gain or loss on the disposal of the asset.

Table 7.15 Journal Entry to Transfer the Cost of Machine A to the Disposal Account

Date	**Account**	**Debit**	**Credit**
31/12/X3	Disposal account	1,000	
31/12/X3	Cost of Machine A		1,000
Being disposal of Machine A for €400 cash			

Table 7.16 Journal Entry to Transfer the Accumulated Depreciation on Machine A to the Disposal Account

Date	**Account**	**Debit**	**Credit**
31/12/X3	Accumulated depreciation on Machine A	300	
31/12/X3	Disposal account		300
Being disposal of Machine A for €400 cash			

Table 7.17 Journal Entry to Record Cash Received for Machine A

Date	Account	Debit	Credit
31/12/X3	Bank	400	
31/12/X3	Disposal account		400

Being disposal of Machine A for €400 cash

Table 7.18

Debit		**Machine A**			Credit
Date	*Account*	*Amount*	*Date*	*Account*	*Amount*
31/12/X3	Balance	1,000	31/12/X3	Disposal	1,000

Debit		**Machine A Accumulated Depreciation**			Credit
Date	*Account*	*Amount*	*Date*	*Account*	*Amount*
31/12/X3	Disposal	300	31/12/X3	Balance	300

Debit		**Bank**			Credit
Date	*Account*	*Amount*	*Date*	*Account*	*Amount*
31/12/X3	Balance	400			
31/12/X3	Disposal	400			

Debit		**Disposal of Machine A**			Credit
Date	*Account*	*Amount*	*Date*	*Account*	*Amount*
31/12/X3	Machine A Cost	1,000	31/12/X3	Bank	400
			31/12/X3	Accumulated depreciation	300
			31/12/X3	Balance	300
		1,000			1,000
31/12/X3	Balance	300			

The balance of €300 on the Disposal of Machine A T Account will be transferred to the Income Statement as an expense item.

Impairment of Receivables

It is common for businesses to sell most of their goods and services on credit. This means that they will carry large amount of receivables on their statements of financial position. These receivables represent the amount due from customers for goods and services supplied to them for which payment has not yet been received. Under IFRS rules receivables are classified as a financial asset which is a contractual right to receive cash or another financial asset from another entity (Figure 7.7).

Figure 7.7
Extract from IAS 32 Financial Instruments: Disclosure and Presentation para. 11

A financial asset is any asset that is:
(a) cash;
...
(c) a contractual right:
 (i) to receive cash or another financial asset from another entity; or ...

Sometimes, there are difficulties in getting paid for goods and services that have been sold on credit. Customers can experience financial difficulties or bankruptcy that can mean that items that are shown as receivables on the statement of financial position will never be received. These amounts are called 'Bad Debts' or 'Impaired Receivables.' Businesses strive to avoid this situation by setting up sophisticated systems of credit control to ensure only financially sound customers receive credit and that overdue amount are followed up promptly. However, even with these systems in place a certain level of bad debts is inevitable.

Figure 7.8 gives an extract from IAS 39 that deals with the impairment of receivables. Paragraph 58 of IAS 39 states that an entity must examine their receivables at the end of each reporting period. This means the entity must access whether the customers are likely to pay their debts. This could be carried out by looking at the age of the receivables to see whether some of them have owed money for a long time. The management of the business should also be aware of whether any of their customers are experiencing financial difficulties. This procedure must be carried out for each financial asset that is individually significant for the business. If there is evidence that some of the receivables may not be able to pay their debts then paragraph 63 of IAS 39 states that these receivables must be 'impaired.' This involves reducing the receivables by the amount that is not expected to be received and charging this amount as an expense in the income statement.

Figure 7.8
Extract from IAS 39 Financial Instruments: Recognition and Measurement

58. An entity shall assess at the end of each reporting period whether there is any objective evidence that a financial asset or group of financial assets is impaired. …

63. If there is objective evidence that an impairment loss on loans and receivables […] has been incurred, the amount of the loss is measured as the difference between the asset's carrying amount and the present value of estimated future cash flows […]. The carrying amount of the asset shall be reduced either directly or through use of an allowance account. The amount of the loss shall be recognised in profit or loss.

Note: This definition has been simplified.

Example

Dingbat ltd. has discovered that one of its customers has gone into liquidation. The customer owed Dingbat Ltd. €2,000 and only €200 is expected to be received from the liquidator. The statement of financial position and income statement of Dingbat Ltd. are given below. The left column shows the financial statements before they have been adjusted for the bad debt. The middle column shows how receivables are impaired by €1,800 and an expense is recorded in the income statement. The right column shows the financial statements after the adjustment is completed.

Table 7.19

Statement of financial position as at 31 December	**31.12.X3**	**Impair-ment**	**After adjustment for impairment**
	€	€	€
Non-Current Assets			
Property, plant & equipment	100,000		100,000
Current Assets			
Inventory	30,000		30,000
Receivables	40,000	1,800 cr	38,200
Cash and cash equivalents	20,000		20,000
Total assets	190,000		188,200
Equity			
Equity share capital	50,000		50,000
Retained Income	140,000		*138,200
	190,000		188,200
Income Statement for the year ended 31 December			
	31.12.X3		**31.12.X3**
	€		€
Revenue	220,000		220,000
Less cost of sales	(160,000)		(160,000)
Gross profit	60,000		60,000
Less expenses			
All expenses (excluding bad debts)	(40,000)		(40,000)
Impairment of receivables	-	1,800 dr	(1,800)
Net profit	20,000		18,200

* Note that retained income has decreased by €1,800 due to the decrease in the net profit in the income statement.

This transaction would be recorded by crediting the receivables account and debiting the impairment of receivables expense account. The receivables account is credited because receivables are an asset and have a debit balance. This account must be credited in order to reduce it. The impairment of receivables expense account is a debit entry like other expense accounts.

Table 7.20 Journal Entry to Record the Impairment of Receivables

Date	Account	Debit	Credit
31/12/X3	Impairment of receivables expense	1,800	
31/12/X3	Receivables		1,800

Being impairment of receivables.

Table 7.21

Debit — **Receivables** — **Credit**

Date	*Account*	*Amount*	*Date*	*Account*	*Amount*
31/12/X3	Balance	40,000	31/12/X3	Impairment of receivables expense	1,800
			31/12/X3	Balance	38,200
		40,000			40,000
31/12/X3	Balance	38,200			

Debit — **Impairment of Receivables Expense** — **Credit**

Date	*Account*	*Amount*	*Date*	*Account*	*Amount*
31/12/X3	Receivables	1,800	31/12/X3	Balance	1,800
		1,800			1,800
31/12/x3	Balance	1,800			

Allowance for Credit Losses

In additional to impairing any individually significant receivables that are not going to be received the business should also look at the large number of smaller receivables that own the entity money. IAS 39 requires the entity to look collectively at 'groups of financial assets with similar credit risk characteristics.' The management will examine variables like the time that the debt has been outstanding, industry and geographical location. The business then uses its past experience with receivables of these types to access what level of allowance for impairment is required for this group of receivables.

An allowance for credit losses is created by recording an expense for the increase in the allowance to income statement. The other side of the entry is to create an allowance account on the statement of financial position. This account is usually subtracted from receivables when preparing the statement of financial position.

Example

Suppose that after a review of its receivables Dingbat Ltd. were to create an allowance for credit losses (AFCL) of €2,100 in 20X4. The financial statements for 20X4 before the allowance was created are given in Table 7.26.

Table 7.26

Statement of financial position as at 31 December	**31.12.X4**	**Creation of Allowance for Credit Losses**	**After Creation of AFCL**
	€	€	€
Non-Current Assets			
Property, plant & equipment	100,000		100,000
Current Assets			
Inventory	32,000		32,000
Receivables	42,000		42,000
Less allowance for credit losses		2,100 cr	(2,100)
Cash and cash equivalents	34,200		34,200
Total assets	208,200		206,100
Equity			
Equity share capital	50,000		50,000
Retained Income	158,200		156,100*
	208,200		206,100

Income Statement for the year ended *31 December*	**31.12.X3**		**31.12.X3**
	€		€
Revenue	220,000		220,000
Less cost of sales	(160,000)		(160,000)
Gross profit	60,000		60,000
Less expenses			
All expenses	(40,000)		(40,000)
Increase in allowance for credit losses		2,100 dr	(2,100)
Net profit	20,000		17,900

* Note that retained income has decreased by €2,100 due to the decrease in the net profit in the income statement.

This increase in the allowance for credit losses is recorded by debiting the income statement with the amount of the increase and crediting the allowance for credit losses account. The credit balance on the allowance for credit losses account offsets the debit balance on the receivables account.

Table 7.27 Journal Entry to Record Increase in the Allowance for Credit Losses

Date	Account	Debit	Credit
31/12/X4	Increase in allowance for credit losses (IS)	2,100	
31/12/X4	Allowance for credit losses (SOFP)		2,100

Being increase in allowance for credit losses

Table 7.28

Debit — Allowance for Credit Losses (SOFP) — Credit

Date	*Account*	*Amount*	*Date*	*Account*	*Amount*
			31/12/X4	Increase in allowance for credit losses	2,100

Debit — Increases in Allowance for Credit Losses (SOFP) — Credit

Date	*Account*	*Amount*	*Date*	*Account*	*Amount*
31/12/X4	Allowance for credit losses	2,100			

Inventory

Inventory is an asset that represents goods that are held for use in the production process or for sale. The IFRS definition of inventory is given in Figure 7.9 below:

Figure 7.9
IFRS Definitions (IAS 2 para 6.)

Inventories are assets:
(a) held for sale in the ordinary course of business;
(b) in the process of production for such sale; or
(c) in the form of materials or supplies to be consumed in the production process or in the rendering of services.

Examples of inventory include finished goods not yet shipped to customers, raw materials not yet converted into finished goods and work-in-progress. Inventories are usually valued at cost price. However if the net realisable value of the inventory falls below the cost price then the inventory must be written down to the net realisable value. Net realisable value is the amount the business expects to receive for the inventory. The IFRS measurement rule and definition of net realisable value is given in Figure 7.10.

Figure 7.10
IFRS Definitions (IAS2 paras. 6 & 9)

Inventories shall be measured at the lower of cost and net realisable value.

Net realisable value is the estimated selling price in the ordinary course of business less the estimated costs of completion and the estimated costs necessary to make the sale.

For example, a business buys in a batch of 100 computers at a cost of €100,000 (€1,000 each.) The business has difficulty finding customers for these computers and three months later at the companies accounting year end 50 of the computers are still in inventory. A new model has been launched during this time and the business expects to be able to sell the computers for €900. In this case, the 50 remaining computers would have to be written down to €900 each. This gives a value for inventory of €45,000 (50 computers x €900 each). The inventory write down is €5,000 (50 computers x €100 each). This write down would be accomplished by debiting a write down of inventory account in the income statement and crediting the inventory account.

Table 7.29 Journal Entry to Write Down Inventory

Date	Account	Debit	Credit
		€	€
31/12/X4	Write-down of inventory (IS)	5,000	
31/12/X4	Inventory (SOFP)		5,000
Being write-down of inventory			

Large businesses keep track of their inventory using sophisticated computer systems. They track arrivals and departures of goods and their costs on a minute by minute basis. Smaller businesses do not usually have such systems. They account for sales and purchases using the invoices they receive from their suppliers and the invoices they send to their customers. Often there is not a perfect match between the amount recorded as sales and purchases in the financial statements and the movements of goods. This necessitates a check on the quantities of inventory using a physical check. This is called stock count. Each item is counted and its cost is established from the accounting records. When all the items are aggregated this gives a figure for closing stock. Some businesses carry out this procedure on a weekly or monthly basis but it must be carried out at least once a year in order to give an accurate inventory figure for the financial statements.

The inventory figure is derived from outside the accounting system. It is not derived from records of purchases or sales that are recorded on an ongoing basis by the bookkeeper. Therefore, it is usually presented separately from the trial balance and must be incorporated into the financial statements as an adjustment.

Conclusion

An asset is a resource that will yield future benefits for the business. Assets are divided into non-current assets and current assets. The economic benefits from property, plant and equipment are used up as it gets older and this must be reflected by depreciating these assets. Current assets usually consist of inventories, receivables and cash balances. Receivables must be reviewed and impaired if there is evidence that they will not all be received. An allowance for credit losses can be established where the firm has groups of receivables that share risk characteristics. Inventory must be valued at the lower of cost and net realisable value.

Chapter 7 Exercises

Exercise 7.1

A Ltd. buys a machine for €50,000. The machine is expected to last 8 years and be worth €10,000 at that time.

(a) Calculate the depreciable amount.

(b) Calculate the annual depreciation charge on the machine.

(c) Calculate the Net Book Value of the asset after 2 years.

Exercise 7.2

The Statement of Financial Position and Income Statement of Acid Ltd.

Statement of financial position as at 31 December	**31.12.X6**	**31.12.X5**	**31.12.X4**
	€	€	€
Non-Current Assets			
Machine A at cost	12,000	12,000	12,000
Machine B at cost	8,000	8,000	
Current Assets			
Bank	26,400	12,900	5,000
Other asset and liabilities	11,100	7,100	10,500
	57,500	40,000	27,500
Equity			
Equity share capital	20,000	20,000	20,000
Retained Income	37,500	20,000	7,500
	57,500	40,000	27,500

Income Statement for the year ended 31 December	**31.12.X6**	**31.12.X5**	**31.12.X4**
	€	€	€
Sales	120,000	110,000	100,000
Less cost of sales	(85,000)	(80,00)	(75,000)
Gross profit	35,000	30,000	25,000
Less expenses			
All expenses (excluding depreciation)	(17,500)	(17,500)	(17,500)
Net profit	17,500	12,500	7,500

The financial statements of Acid Ltd. show three years of information. The first year ended 31 December 19X4 is on the right most side of the table. On the 1st of January 19X4 Acid purchased a machine (Machine A) for €12,000. They estimate this machine will last 6 years and have to be scrapped at that point. On the 1st of January 19X5 Acid still had this machine and purchased a second machine (Machine B) for €8,000. This machine will last 6 years and be worth €2,000 at that point. The company uses straight-line depreciation.

No depreciation has been recorded in the financial statements.

(a) Calculate the depreciation for Machine A & B. Record this depreciation in the financial statements using the template supplied.

The Statement of financial position and Income Statement of Acid Ltd. With depreciation

Statement of financial position as at 31 December	**31.12.X6**	**31.12.X5**	**31.12.X4**
	€	€	€
Non-Current Assets			
Machine A at cost	12,000	12,000	12,000
Accumulated depreciation on machine A			
Net Book Value (NBV) of machine A			
Machine B at cost	8,000	8,000	
Accumulated depreciation on machine B			
Net Book Value (NBV) of machine A			
Total non-current assets			
Current Assets			
Bank	26,400	12,900	5,000
Other asset and liabilities	11,100	7,100	10,500
Equity			
Equity share capital	20,000	20,000	20,000
Retained Income			

Income Statement for the year ended 31 December	**31.12.X6**	**31.12.X5**	**31.12.X4**
	€	€	€
Sales	120,000	110,000	100,000
Less cost of sales	(85,000)	(80,00)	(75,000)
Gross profit	35,000	30,000	25,000
Less expenses			
Depreciation on machine A			
Depreciation on machine B			
All expenses (excluding depreciation)	(17,500)	(17,500)	(17,500)

Net profit

(b) Show the journal entries for depreciation in each of the three years

20x4
Machine A

Date	Account	Debit	Credit

Being

20x5
Machine A

Date	Account	Debit	Credit

Being

Machine B

Date	Account	Debit	Credit

Being

20x6
Machine A

Date	Account	Debit	Credit

Being

Machine B

Date	Account	Debit	Credit

Being

(c) Prepare the Cost of Machine A T account, Accumulated Depreciation on Machine A T account and the Depreciation on Machine A expense T account for 20x4.

Debit — **Cost of Machine A (SOFP)** — **Credit**

Date	*Account*	*Amount*	*Date*	*Account*	*Amount*

Debit — **Accumulated Depreciation on Machine A (SOFP)** — **Credit**

Date	*Account*	*Amount*	*Date*	*Account*	*Amount*

Debit — **Depreciation Expense on Machine A (IS)** — **Credit**

Date	*Account*	*Amount*	*Date*	*Account*	*Amount*

(d) On 31.12.X6 the company disposes of Machine A for €6,500 in cash. Record this transaction in the spreadsheet below.

Statement of financial position as at 31 December	**31.12.X6**	**Disposal**	**After Disposal**
	€	€	€
Non-Current Assets			
Machine A at cost	12,000		
Accumulated depreciation on machine A	(6,000)		
Net Book Value (NBV) of machine A	6,000		
Machine B at cost	8,000		
Accumulated depreciation on machine B	(2,000)		
Net Book Value (NBV) of machine B	6,000		
Total non-current assets	12,000		
Current Assets			
Bank	26,400		
Other asset and liabilities	11,100		
	49,500		
Equity			
Equity share capital	20,000		
Retained Income (op 15,000 +14,500)	29,500		
	49,500		

Income Statement for the year ended 31 December	**31.12.X6**	**Disposal**	**After Disposal**
	€	€	€
Sales	120,000		
Less cost of sales	(85,000)		
Gross profit	35,000		
Less expenses			
Depreciation on machine A	(2,000)		
Depreciation on machine B	(1,000)		
Profit on sale of machine			
All expenses (excluding depreciation)	(17,500)		
Net profit	14,500		

(e) Prepare the journal entries for the disposal of machine A

Date	Account	Debit	Credit

Being

Date	Account	Debit	Credit

Being

Date	Account	Debit	Credit

Being

(f) Prepare the disposal account for Machine A

Debit		**Cost of Machine A (SOFP)**			**Credit**
Date	*Account*	*Amount*	*Date*	*Account*	*Amount*

Debit		**Accumulated Depreciation on Machine A (SOFP)**			**Credit**
Date	*Account*	*Amount*	*Date*	*Account*	*Amount*

Debit		**Bank (SOFP)**			**Credit**
Date	*Account*	*Amount*	*Date*	*Account*	*Amount*

Debit		**Disposal of Machine A (SOFP)**			**Credit**
Date	*Account*	*Amount*	*Date*	*Account*	*Amount*

Exercise 7.3

Dodgy Ltd. has a receivables balance of €1,000,000. It becomes aware that one of its customers is having financial difficulties. This customer owes €20,000 and none of this amount is likely to be recovered.

(a) Prepare a journal entry to impair the receivable

Date	Account	Debit	Credit

Being

(b) The management of Dodgy Ltd. decide to create an allowance for credit losses of €49,000 of receivables. Prepare a journal to record this transaction

Date	Account	Debit	Credit

Being

(c) What figure will appear for receivables in Dodgy's statement of financial position?

(d) What figure will be expensed for bad debts in Dodgy's income statement?

Exercise 7.4

The following data relates to questions 1, 2 and 3.

Trial Balance (extract) for the year ended 31.12 X6:

	Debit €	Credit €
Receivables	100,000	
Impairment of receivables expense	2,000	
Allowance for credit losses		1,000
Revenue		1,005,000

At the end of the year it was discovered that a major customer of the business had gone into liquidation. They will only be able to pay €1,000 of the amount owing of €10,000. After a review of the remaining receivables it was decided to adjust the allowance for credit losses to a new figure of €4,550.

1. The balance on the allowance for credit losses account will amount to:

a) €4,500
b) €4,550
c) €5,000
d) €4,900
e) None of the above.

2. What is the impairment of receivables expense that will appear in the company's income statement, for the year ended 31.12.X6?

a) €14,000
b) €12,000
c) €2,000
d) €10,000
e) None of the above

3. The amount for receivables that will appear in the company's statement of financial position is:

a) €87,450
b) €98,000
c) €97,000
d) €86,450
e) None of the above

4. A garage sold its air pump and bought a new model on 1/1/X6. The old air pump had been purchased on 1/1/X4 and had been depreciated on a 25% straight line basis. The air pump that was sold had cost €1,200 and was sold for €300. The profit/(loss) on disposal of the old air pump was:

a) €600 profit
b) €600 loss
c) €300 profit
d) €300 loss
e) None of the above

5. Straight Line Ltd. purchased a machine on 1 January 20X3 for €60,000. It estimated that the machine would have a useful life of 10 years and a residual value of €10,000. Calculate the accumulated depreciation on the machine at 31 December 20X4.

a) €5,000
b) €6,000
c) €10,000
d) €12,000
e) None of the above

6. Straight Line Ltd. purchased a machine on 1 January 2000 for €40,000. It estimated that the machine would have a useful life of 10 years and a residual value of €10,000. Calculate the accumulated depreciation on the machine at 31 December 2001.

a) €4,000
b) €6,000
c) €9,000
d) €12,000
e) None of the above

7. The following information pertaining to a cutting machine is available:

	€
Acquisition cost	59,000
Estimated residual value	1,250
Expected life	10 years

If the firm uses straight-line depreciation, what is the balance in the accumulated depreciation account at the end of the third year of the machine's expected life?

a) €17,700
b) €11,800
c) €5,900
d) €17,325
e) €11,550

Chapter 8

Equity

Introduction

Equity is the residual interest in the assets of the entity after deducting all its liabilities. A business might have assets of €1,000,000 and liabilities of €600,000. This would leave equity of €400,000. If that business were to be liquidated then there should be €400,000[23] available to be distributed to the shareholders. Shareholders usually hold the residual interest in a limited company. This means that they get to keep what ever is left over after everybody else is paid off.

Sources of Finance

A business requires an investment in order to get started and to operate. This investment typically comes from either shareholders or from borrowing. These two sources of finance differ in three main ways from the company's perspective.

Firstly, shareholders cannot withdraw the funds that they have invested in the company[24]. Even when a firm is doing badly shareholders can only try to sell their shares to another investor they can not ask the company to refund their money. Because of this, share capital is considered the permanent capital of the business. In contrast to this, when a company borrows money a schedule of repayments is agreed. This may involve paying the interest and capital back evenly over the life of the loan or repayment of interest and capital can be deferred to the end of the loan. Should the company not be able to meet a loan repayment the loan agreement usually specifies that the full amount of the loan becomes payable immediately. This means that borrowing is more risky from the company's perspective. If they encounter financial difficulty and cannot meet loan repayments the bank usually have the right to appoint a receiver and

---

[23] This ignores the cost of liquidation and assumes that all the assets and liabilities can be turned into their statement of financial position values.

[24] There are provisions for companies 're-purchasing' shares. These provisions are usually used where the company has excess resources that they want to distribute back to the shareholders.

take any assets that they have security over. At the very least the borrower will have to re-negotiate their loan with the bank which is a costly process.

Secondly, shareholders do not receive a fixed return on their investment in the business. They are the residual claimants and will only receive dividends where there are funds available after paying off other claimants and where the directors think it is a good idea to pay dividends. In contrast to this, banks receive either a fixed interest rate on their lending or a variable rate that is tied to a base rate. Interest must be paid according to the agreed schedule and if the firm is not able to pay they face receivership or re-negotiation of the loan.

Thirdly, shareholders have little protection if the company has financial difficulties. Shareholders are the residual claimants on the company's assets. If liabilities exceed the assets then there will be nothing left to pay out to the shareholders. Lenders have considerably better right in the case of financial distress. If the company misses loan payments lenders can usually take control of assets that have been pledged as security.

Statements of financial position of Limited Companies

The equity section of the statement of financial position shows how the businesses equity is made up. The distinctions between different types of equity and how they are presented often depends on company law provisions.

Equity share capital

Company law allows the capital of a company to be divided into shares. When a company is set up it must specify a unit for these shares. Figure 8.1 shows the Companies Act, 1963 requirement to state this amount in the Memorandum of Association. This 'fixed amount' that the capital is divided into is called the 'par value' or the 'nominal value' of the shares. This can be set at any amount but is usually set at €1.00.

Figure 8.1
Companies Act, 1963
Part II Incorporation of Companies and Matters Incidental Thereto
Memorandum of Association

6 Requirements in relation to memorandum

(1) The memorandum of every company must state -
...
(4) In the case of a company having a share capital -
(a) the memorandum must also, ..., state the amount of share capital with which the company proposes to be registered, and the division thereof into shares of a fixed amount;

The company's equity share capital is the par value of the company's shares multiplied by the number of shares that have been issued.

Shares in the capital of a company can be either preference or ordinary. Ordinary shares are included under the statement of financial position heading 'Equity share capital.' Ordinary shareholders have a number of rights. Firstly, they have limited liability. This means that they can only lose their investment in the company. If the company's liabilities exceed its assets then they cannot be asked to contribute to meet the deficit[25]. Secondly, they are entitled to receive any ordinary dividends that are paid by the company. Dividends on ordinary shares can only be paid when the funds are available and where the directors feel that it is appropriate to pay dividends. Thirdly, the company's directors are elected by the ordinary shareholders. Each share has one vote in such elections. If the ordinary shareholders are dissatisfied with the management of the company they can replace the directors. Ordinary shareholders can also vote on major decisions that the company has to take like acquisitions and issue of further share capital.

Example

Joanne Hughes wished to set up a limited company to trade as a newsagent. She prepares the Memorandum and Articles of Association and specifies a par

---

[25] If the shareholder was involved in the management of the company and had engaged in any wrongdoing this may not be the case. This is called 'lifting the veil' of limited liability. Also the shareholders in many small companies are asked to provide personal guarantees of any lending by the company. This negates the effect of limited liability.

value of €1 for each share. The company is to be called Gonzo Ltd. She subscribes for 1,000 shares of €1 each by writing a personal cheque to Gonzo Ltd. This cheque can then be lodged to Gonzo's bank account. The statement of financial position of Gonzo would be prepared as below after the issue of shares.

Table 8.1

Statement of financial position	**Company Formed** €	**Issue of share capital** €	**After issue of share capital** €
Current Assets			
Cash and cash equivalents	0	1,000 dr	1,000
Total assets	0		1,000
Equity			
Equity share capital	0	1,000 cr	1,000
Retained Income	0		0
	0		1,000

The journal entry for this issue of shares is to debit bank and credit equity share capital.

Table 8.2 Journal Entry to Record Issue of Shares

Date	**Account**	**Debit**	**Credit**
…	Bank	1,000	
…	Equity share capital		1,000
Being issue of shares			

Table 8.3

Debit — **Bank** — **Credit**

Date	*Account*	*Amount*	*Date*	*Account*	*Amount*
…	Equity share capital	1,000			

Debit — **Equity Share Capital** — **Credit**

Date	*Account*	*Amount*	*Date*	*Account*	*Amount*
			…	Bank	1,000

Preference share capital

Preference shares differ from ordinary shares in three main ways. Firstly, preference shareholders are not residual claimants on the business. If the business were shut down they would be repaid the par value of their shareholding and would not share in any extra assets that had been accumulated in the business. Any excess of assets over liabilities and preference share capital would be distributed to the ordinary shareholders. Secondly, they receive a pre-determined rate of dividends on their capital. For example, 8% preference shares with a par value of €1 would receive a dividend of €0.08 per share each year. There is an important difference between preference shares and a bank loan in this respect. The dividend on preference shares can only be paid when the company has sufficient funds. If the company cannot pay the dividend it is skipped. If the preference share are 'cumulative' then the company must pay skipped dividends when it is able. Thirdly, preference shares can be 'redeemable' in which case the par value of the shares can be paid back to the shareholders.

Share premium

Companies can issue shares for more than their par values. Any excess over the par value that a company receives for the issue or shares is known as 'Share Premium.' Figure 8.2 gives the Companies Act, 1963 requirement in relation to share premium. Share premium is shown separately from equity share capital on the statement of financial position.

Figure 8.2
Companies Act, 1963
Part III Share Capital and Debentures
Issues of Shares at Premium and Discount and Redeemable Preference Shares

62 Application of premiums received on issue of shares.

(1) Where a company issues shares at a premium, whether for cash or otherwise, a sum equal to the aggregate amount or value of the premiums on those shares shall be transferred to an account, to be called "the share premium account",...

Example

The director's of Gonzo Ltd. Decide to issue another 500 shares. These shares will be issued at €1.10. The effect of this transaction on Gonzo Ltd.'s statement of financial position is shown below.

Table 8.4

Statement of financial position	**Before Issue**	**Issue of share capital at €1.10**	**After issue of share capital**
	€	€	€
Current Assets			
Cash and cash equivalents	1,000	550 dr	1,550
Total assets	1,000		1,550
Equity			
Equity share capital	1,000	500 cr	1,500
Share premium		50 cr	50
Retained Income	0		0
	1,000		1,550

The journal entry for this issue of shares is to debit bank with the amount of cash received from the shareholders. Equity share capital is then credited with the par value of the shares and share premium is credited with any excess over the par value.

Table 8.5 Journal Entry to Record Issue of Shares

Date	**Account**	**Debit**	**Credit**
...	Bank	550	
...	Equity share capital		500
	Share premium		50
Being issue of shares			

Table 8.6

Debit		Bank			Credit
Date	*Account*	*Amount*	*Date*	*Account*	*Amount*
...	Equity share capital	500			
	Share premium	50			

Debit		Equity Share Capital			Credit
Date	*Account*	*Amount*	*Date*	*Account*	*Amount*
			...	Bank	500

Debit		Share Premium			Credit
Date	*Account*	*Amount*	*Date*	*Account*	*Amount*
			...	Bank	50

Retained income

Equity is composed of two main parts. Firstly, the contributed capital of the company has been described above. This consists of the amount of money received from the shareholders. It is equal to equity share capital plus share premium. Secondly, as the company starts to trade it will increase its net assets by engaging in favourable trade and making a profit. In this way the equity of the business will be increased without the shareholders contributing any extra funds. Consider the effect on the accounting equation of the company buying some goods for €100 and immediately selling them for €200.

Figure 8.3
The Accounting Equation

Assets – Liabilities	= Equity
+100	+100

Equity would increase by €100 even though the shareholders have not contributed any extra capital. We can call this the 'internally generated' capital of the company. It is measured by the profit or loss from the period in the income statement. This amount is transferred from the income statement to the retained income account in the statement of financial position at the end of each year. The retained income account is equal to the accumulated profit[26] of the business since it was set up.

Retained income is considered to be a part of the shareholders investment in the company and is therefore included when we calculate ratios like the debt/equity percentage or return on equity.

Total Equity

The company's total equity is equal to the sum of equity share capital plus share premium plus retained income. The last item is internally generated capital while the first two items have been contributed by the shareholders in cash. This relationship is show in Figure 8.4.

Figure 8.4
Total Equity

Equity Share Capital
+
Preference Share Capital
+
Share Premium
+
Retained Income
=
Total Equity

Dividends

Dividends are the return to owning shares in a company. Dividends can be paid at any time during the financial year but it is usual to pay an interim divided after the announcement of half yearly results[27] and a final dividend after the announcement of the financial statement for the financial year. Dividends can only be out of retained income. This means that the company must have

---

[26] Dividends are subtracted from the retained income account each year. Under IFRS this is shown in the movements in equity statement.

[27] Companies listed on the UK or Irish stock exchange are required to produce interim financial statement half yearly. These financial statements are not audited. In the US listed companies produce quarterly interim financial statements.

enough current and retained profits to pay the dividend[28]. Dividends cannot be paid out of the contributed equity of the company. These rules date back to the earliest company law. In a limited company borrowers worry that any money they advance to the company will be paid out as a dividend rather than being invested in the company. These rules help to reassure borrowers that shareholders can only withdraw profits as dividends.

Dividends are not shown on the face of the income statement. They are shown in the notes to the financial statements as a movement on the retained income account. Only dividends that have actually been paid are recorded in the financial statements. Dividends that have been proposed by the directors of the company are noted in the financial statements but not recorded.

Example a company pays an ordinary dividend of €0.10 per €1.00 share. There are 100,000 shares in issue. The total dividend is €10,000 (100,000 shares x €0.10.)

Table 8.7 Journal Entry to Record Payment of Dividends

Date	Account	Debit	Credit
...	Retained income	10,000	
...	Bank		10,000
Being payment of dividend			

Table 8.8

Debit			Bank		Credit
Date	*Account*	*Amount*	*Date*	*Account*	*Amount*
			...	Retained income	10,000

Debit			Retained Income		Credit
Date	*Account*	*Amount*	*Date*	*Account*	*Amount*
...	Bank	10,000			

[28] The rules governing the payment of dividends are contained in the Companies Acts. They are much more complex than is suggested by the above statement.

Transfer of Shares

Once a company has issued shares these shares can be transferred from the person to whom they were originally issued to another person or company. This is called a secondary market. A stock exchange is an example of a secondary market. For small companies shares can be sold directly from one person to another. The price at which a company's shares are transferred at is not usually significant for the company's statement of financial position. This is because the company does not get any of the money that is involved in the transfer. The legal position is that the company sells a share of its capital. This share is then the asset of an individual and they can dispose of it as they see fit.

Summary

The shareholders' residual interest in the company is called equity. Equity is divided into equity share capital, share premium and retained income.

Chapter 8 Exercises

Exercise 8.1

(a) Name the sources of finance that are available to the business?

(b) Rank the sources of finance from the riskiest (from the firm's point of view) to the least risky.

(c) Loads-a-money Ltd. has issued the following securities

10,000 ordinary shares of €1 each
5,000 preference shares of €2 each
A long term loan of €20,000

Loads-a-money has retained income of €50,000.

Draft the 'Equity' and 'Non-current Assets' section of the statement of financial position.

Exercise 8.2

Questions 1, 2 and 3 are based on the following information

The following is an extract from Singsong's statement of financial position: -

Statement of financial position of Singsong plc. as at 31/12/X7

	€	€
Non-current assets		
Premises		400,000
Current assets		
Inventory	230,000	
Receivables	50,000	
Bank	20,000	
Total current assets		300,000
		700,000
Equity		
Equity share capital		230,000
Retained income		370,000
		600,000
Current liabilities		
Payables		100,000
		700,000

1. Given only the information above, which of the following statements appears true?

a) The shareholders have contributed €600,000 to the business in cash as share capital.
b) The shareholders have contributed €230,000 in cash to the business.
c) The shareholders have taken profits of €370,000 out of the business.
d) The shareholders have contributed €370,000 in ordinary share capital to the business.
e) None of the above.

2. If Singsong's shareholders were to contribute a further €30,000 in share capital the financed section of statement of financial position would change to the following: -

a)

Equity

Equity share capital	230,000
Retained income	370,000
	600,000

b)

Equity

Equity share capital	230,000
Retained income	400,000
	630,000

c)

Equity

Equity share capital	260,000
Retained income	370,000
	630,000

d)

Equity

Equity share capital	260,000
Retained income	400,000
	660,000

e) None of the above.

3. Which of the following statements is true?

a) Singsong's assets are €300,000
b) Singsong's assets are €200,000
c) Singsong's liabilities are €200,000
d) Singsong's liabilities are €600,000
e) None of the above is true

Exercise 8.3

K consultants are set up by Kim, Kate, Kevin & Keanu. The company has authorised share capital of 100,000 ordinary shares of €1 each and 20,000 10% preference shares of €1 each. They invest in the new business as follows:-

Kim buys 20,000 ordinary shares for €30,000.
Kate buys 30,000 ordinary shares for €45,000.
Kevin lends €10,000 which will have to be repaid in 10 years time along with interest at 5%.
Keanu buys 10,000 preference shares for €10,000.

(a) Use the grid provided to show how each transaction is recorded.
(b) Draft journal entries for each of the transactions.
(c) Draft the statement of financial position after all the transactions have been completed.

	Kim	Kate	Kevin	Keanu	Sum Across
Assets					
Bank					
Equity					
Equity share capital – Preference shares					
Equity share capital – Ordinary shares					
Share premium					
Total equity					
Non-current liabilities					
Long term debt					

Exercise 8.4

Questions 1 to 3 are based on the following information:

Extract from the statement of financial position of Moe Ltd.

As at	31/12/x2	31/12/x1
	€'000	€'000
Long term debt	1,000	750
Equity share capital - Ordinary shares of €.75 each	1,500	750
Share premium	350	100
Retained income	1,241	953

1. The 'Total Equity' at 31/12/x2 for Moe Ltd. is: -
a) €4,091,000.
b) €3,091,000.
c) €1,850,000.
d) €1,500,000.
e) None of the above.

2. The number of ordinary shares in issue at 31/12/x2 is: -
a) 750,000.
b) 1,500,000.
c) 2,000,000.
d) 2,250,000.
e) None of the above.

3. One issue of ordinary shares was made during the year ended 31/12/x2. All of the shares were sold at the same price. Select the price at which the shares were issued:

a) €1.00.
b) €1.25.
c) €0.75.
d) €2.00.
e) None of the above.

Exercise 8.5 - MiniCase

Dublin Investment Bank plc

"The re-capitalisation of Dublin Investment Bank will provide new capital for organic growth and safeguard its future as a dynamic Irish Investment Bank."
Jim Murphy, CEO DIB.

Dublin Investment Bank [DIB] is a large indigenous bank that specializes in lending to medium and large Irish companies. These companies are mainly in the construction, leisure and services sectors of the economy. It is based in Dublin with branches in Cork, Limerick and London. Since the 1970s it has grown quickly as it can provide more tailored financial solutions to its clients than the larger financial institutions.

The Board of Directors of DIB consider that in order to finance future growth they must raise more finance. They intend to raise €450m. They will use the new finance to make more loans to both their existing clients and new clients. They are considering a number of options which are given in Table 1.

Table 1
Possible sources of finance

(a) Issue new ordinary shares. The market price of existing shares is €10.00 each and they would probably have to offer a 10% discount to the market to take up the new shares. This would involve selling the shares at a price of Euro 9.00 each.

(b) Enter into an agreement to borrow money from another bank at a 3.5% rate of interest. This loan would have to be repaid in one repayment in 10 years time. Interest would be paid monthly.

(c) Issue preference shares. DIB has 1,000m authorised 5% preference shares with a par value of €1 each.

You have been hired as a consultant and you must advise the bank on the following issues:

(a) The risks and returns associated with the sources of finance in Table 1.

(b) The effects on the statement of financial position of the sources of finance above.

Dr John McCallig of UCD Dublin prepared this case. It is based on a fictional situation.

(c) The accounting journal entries (Debit-Credit) necessary to record each of the sources of finance above.

See Exhibit 1 and ignore the effects of taxation.

Exhibit 1

The 'Financed by' section of the bank's statement of financial position is as follows:

As at	**31/12/05 €m**	**31/12/04 €m**
Non-current liabilities		
Long term debt	920	720
Equity		
Equity share capital		
- 5% Irredeemable preference shares of €1 each	0	0
- Ordinary shares of €2.50 each	300	250
Share premium	375	250
Retained income	120	80
	795	580
	1,715	1,300

Chapter 9

Liabilities

Introduction

According to IFRS, a liability is a present obligation of the entity arising from past events, the settlement of which is expected to result in an outflow from the entity of resources embodying economic benefits.

Liabilities represent outflows form the business in the future. Examples of liabilities include payables, taxation due and borrowings.

Current and Non-current Liabilities

Liabilities are divided into current and non-current depending on when they will result in an outflow. The IFRS definition is given in Figure 9.1.

Figure 9.1
IFRS definitions

60. A liability shall be classified as current when it satisfies any of the following criteria:

(a) it is expected to be settled in the entity's normal operating cycle;
(b) it is held primarily for the purpose of being traded;
(c) it is due to be settled within twelve months after the statement of financial position date; or
(d) the entity does not have an unconditional right to defer settlement of the liability for at least twelve months after the statement of financial position date.

All other liabilities shall be classified as non-current.

Payables

Most businesses buy their raw materials or finished goods on credit. This means they take delivery of the goods immediately but only pay for them in the future. Companies typically grant credit terms of 30 days. However, in Ireland many firms take considerably longer than this to settle their obligations. The payables figure on the statement of financial position represents the amount that the business owes to its suppliers.

Corporation Tax

Companies are liable to corporation tax on their profits. Corporation tax is assessed on the profits of companies for accounting periods. For example if a company's accounting year ends on 31/3/06, corporation tax would be accessed on this period's profit. This contrasts with income tax which is accessed on the income of individuals and always accessed on calendar year periods (1 January – 31 December). The main rate of corporation tax is 12.5%[29]. This is the standard rate of corporation tax on income from the company's trade or profession. Corporation tax must be paid in two instalments. 90% of the corporation tax liability for each year is due is payable not later than the 21st day of the month preceding the end of the accounting period[30]. This means for a company with a 31/12/06 year end it must work out an estimate of its corporation tax for the year to 31/12/06 in November 2006 and pay 90% of this amount by 21/11/06. The remaining balance in paid within nine months of the end of the accounting period[31].

Corporation tax is calculated by taking the profit of the company, adding back any expenses not allowable and subtracting any expenses that are allowed for tax purposes but not allowed when calculating the accounting profit. A sample corporation tax calculation is shown in figure 9.2.

---

[29] There are other rates of corporation tax for specialised situations. 25%: Non-trading income [includes income chargeable under Case III (e.g. discounts, interest, and foreign income), Case IV (patent royalties, miscellaneous income) & Case V (rental income from land & buildings in the State) of Schedule D]. Also included at this rate is income from activities which consist of working minerals, petroleum activities & dealing in or developing land, other than construction operations. 10%: Certain companies have their profits taxed at an effective rate of 10%. This 'manufacturing rate' is in the process of being phased out but remains in existence for some companies until 2010. See www.revenue.ie for more details.

[30] Companies with a corporation tax liability of more than €200,000 in their previous accounting period will now be obliged to pay their preliminary tax in two instalments. A first instalment will be payable in the sixth month of the accounting period and the amount payable should equal 50% of the final total liability for the prior period or 45% of the total estimated liability for the current period. The second instalment will be due in the eleventh month and should bring the total preliminary tax payment up to 90% of the final corporation tax liability for the current accounting period. These measures are effective for accounting periods commencing on or after 14 October 2008.

[31] The payment is due on the 21st day of the month preceding the ninth month after the end of the accounting period.

Figure 9.2
Corporation Tax Calculation

Profit per income statement

Add back any disallowed expenses (which have been allowed in the income Statement)
- Items of capital expenditure.
- Expenditure not wholly and exclusively laid out of the purposes of the trade.
- Private expenditure of company directors/employees.
- Losses not connected with the trade for example betting losses by the taxpayer
- Only specific impairments of receivables are allowed (not increases in a allowance for credit losses.)
- Accounting depreciation.
- Speculative losses on the stock exchange.
- Charitable and political contributions.
- Entertainment expenses.
- Motor expenses are restricted.
- Interest fines on late tax.
- Speeding/parking fines.

Less Expenses Allowed (which have not been allowed in the income statement)
- Bona fida director's salaries and fees *are* allowable as an expense of the company.
- Interest on loans taken out to finance the trade.
- Goods stolen.

Less capital allowances

= Taxable profits

Accounting depreciation is not allowed as a tax expense. However, capital allowances are a tax deductible allowance for wear and tear on assets. The rate available on assets is given in Figure 9.2. All of these allowances are calculated using the straight line method.

Figure 9.2
Rates of Capital Allowances

Plant & machinery	12.5%
Motor vehicles (restricted)	12.5%
Industrial buildings	4%

Accounting for Corporation Tax

One month before the end of the accounting year (e.g. 31/12/2006) the company's tax advisers will have worked out the estimated corporation tax for 2006. The company will pay 90% of this estimate one month before the year end and the balance 9 months after the year end. However, the company will include the full amount of corporation tax in 2006's accounts. This means that the profit for the year and the full tax on that profit appear in the same set of accounts.

Example

Bling Ltd.'s accounting year ends on 31/12/06. Its profit before tax was €40,000 and the Corporation tax is estimated at €4,500. It paid €4,050 on 21/11/06 and €450 on 21/8/07.

On 21/11/06 when the tax expense is worked out, it is recorded as an expense in the income statement and as a liability in the statement of financial position.

Table 9.1 Journal Entry to Record Tax Expense for 2006

Date	Account	Debit	Credit
21/11/06	Tax expense (IS)	4,500	
21/11/06	Tax liability (BS)		4,500
Being tax expense.			

Table 9.2 Bling Ltd. Income Statement for the year ended 31/12/06

	€
Profit before tax	40,000
Tax expense	(4,500)
Profit for the financial year	35,500

On 21/11/06 the company will have to pay off some of its Corporation Tax

Table 9.3 Journal Entry to Record Payment of Preliminary Tax

Date	Account	Debit	Credit
21/11/06	Tax liability (BS)	4,050	
21/11/06	Bank (BS)		4,050

Being payment of preliminary tax

Corporation tax will be paid in 1 more payments in the following year (2007)
On 21/8/07

Table 9.4 Journal Entry to Record Payment of Balance of Tax Due

Date	Account	Debit	Credit
21/8/07	Tax liability (BS)	450	
21/8/07	Bank (BS)		450

The company must file a corporation tax return at the same time as making the final corporation tax payment. When the revenue commissioners receive the company's corporation tax return they may disagree with some of the figures. If the final tax liability differs from that originally estimated and included in the 2006 accounts then any differences are included with next year's (2007's) tax charge. For example, if the final liability agreed with the revenue was €4,750 then €250 (4,750-4,500) would be included in 2007's tax charge.

Accounting for Value Added Tax (VAT)

Value Added Tax (VAT) is a turnover tax, charged on goods sold and supplied within Ireland and on goods exported to other EU members. Businesses must register for VAT unless their turnover (revenue) is less than prescribed limits[32]. Businesses smaller than the prescribed limits can register for VAT if they wish. When a business registers it receives a VAT Number. This is a permanent identifier that is used in the VAT system. Each business registered for VAT will charge VAT at the appropriate rate on its sales of goods and services. The main rates of VAT are given in Figure 9.3.

[32] Details on the revenue limits for VAT registration are available at www.revenue.ie

Figure 9.3
VAT Rates

Exempt	Education, Medical services, Banks
0%	Food & Drink, Medicines, Books, Children's clothes
13.5%	Construction, Agriculture, Waste Disposal, Cinemas, Hotels, Fuel (not petrol)
21.5%	Luxury Goods

When a business makes a sale it raised a VAT invoice and sends this invoice to its customer. Figure 9.4 details the information that is required on a VAT invoice.

Figure 9.4
Information required on a VAT sales invoice

- Name and address of issuer
- VAT Number
- Name and address of customer
- Description of goods or services
- VAT Rate and amount

Businesses are allowed to claim a deduction from their VAT liability for the VAT they have paid on their purchases. This is called an 'Input Credit.' Businesses do not receive an Input Credit for the purchase of motor cars, petrol and entertainment. A business must have a valid VAT invoice from its suppliers for each item that it claims as an input credit.

The VAT system is illustrated in Table 9.5. This example assumes that the goods attract a VAT rate of 21%. A manufacturer produces goods and sells them for €100. The VAT payable on this transaction is €21.50 (€100 x 21.5%) and the price charged to the distributor is €121.50 (€100 + €21.50 VAT). The distributor re-sells the goods for €150. The distributor will charge VAT of €32.25 (€150 x 21.5%) on this transaction giving a sales price of €182.25 (€150 + €32.25). The distributor had paid the manufacturer €121.50 for the goods. This price includes €21.50 of VAT that the distributor can set against the VAT on sales. This input credit of €21.50 is deducted from the €32.25 VAT charged on the sale to give €10.75 of VAT which has to be paid over to the Revenue Commissioners. The retailer pays over the VAT they receive from the consumer (€47.30) minus the VAT they paid to the distributor (€32.25). The consumer is not able to re-claim VAT on goods that they consume and they have to pay the VAT on these goods over to the retailer. In this way, VAT is collected at each step in the chain for goods and services. The final consumer pays VAT of €47.30 and bears all of this cost. The manufacturer, distributor and retailer collect the VAT as the goods pass through their business but they do not bear the cost of this tax.

Table 9.5 The VAT System

	Purchase price (incl. VAT)	VAT On Purchases	Sales	Vat on Sales	Total Sales price	VAT paid
	€	€	€	€	€	€
Manufacturer	0.00	0.00	100.00	21.50	121.50	21.50
Distributor	121.50	21.50	150.00	32.25	182.25	10.75
Retailer	182.25	32.25	220.00	47.30	267.30	15.05
Consumer	267.30	47.30				
Total						**47.30**

The year is divided into six 2 month VAT periods[33]. Each VAT registered business has to fill in the form and return it with a cheque by the 19th day of the month following the VAT period. Each business calculates the VAT that is due using the formula in Figure 9.5.

Figure 9.5
Calculation of VAT due to the Revenue

VAT on Revenue

-

VAT on Expenses (input credits)

=

VAT due to the Revenue Commissioners

In the income statement revenue and expenses[34] are shown exclusive of VAT. This is because businesses collect VAT on behalf of the revenue commissioners and pay this VAT over. The VAT does not constitute a revenue or expense of

[33] There are now provisions for paying VAT on an annual basis.
[34] Expenses on which VAT cannot be reclaimed should be shown including VAT as this VAT cannot be reclaimed and constitutes a cost of the business.

the business. In the statement of financial position non-current assets[35] and inventory are also shown excluding VAT. Again, this is because VAT on the acquisition of assets can be reclaimed as an input credit and does not constitute an asset of the business. The VAT liability owed to the revenue commissioners at the statement of financial position date should be recorded as a current liability.

For example, a business buys goods for €121.50 including VAT (€100 + €21.50 VAT) and sells them for €145.80 (€120 + €25.80 VAT). The purchase is recorded as follows:

Table 9.6 Journal Entry to Record a Purchase of Goods (with VAT)

Date	Account	Debit	Credit
...	Purchases	100.00	
...	VAT liability	21.50	
...	Bank		121.50
Being purchase of goods			

The bank accounting is reduced by the VAT inclusive amount of the purchase because this is the amount that must be paid to the supplier. Purchases are increased by the VAT exclusive amount because expenses are shown VAT exclusive. The amount of VAT is debited to the VAT liability account where it will be offset against the VAT on sales to give the amount due for VAT. The sale transaction is recorded as follows:

Table 9.7 Journal Entry to Record a Sale of Goods (with VAT)

Date	Account	Debit	Credit
...	Bank	145.80	
...	Revenue		120.00
...	VAT liability		45.80
Being sale of goods			

The bank account is increased by €145.80 which is the VAT inclusive amount which is received from the customer. Revenue is increased by the VAT exclusive amount because revenues are shown exclusive of VAT. The VAT on the sale increases the VAT liability and is therefore credited to the VAT liability account.

[35] VAT on motor cars cannot be treated as an input credit and should be counted as part of the cost of the asset.

Table 9.8 shows these transactions after the have been posted to T accounts.

Table 9.8

Debit		**Bank**			**Credit**
Date	*Account*	*Amount*	*Date*	*Account*	*Amount*
...	Revenue/VAT	145.80	...	Purchases/VAT	121.50

Debit		**Revenue**			**Credit**
Date	*Account*	*Amount*	*Date*	*Account*	*Amount*
			...	Bank	120.00

Debit		**Purchases**			**Credit**
Date	*Account*	*Amount*	*Date*	*Account*	*Amount*
...	Bank	100.00			

Debit		**VAT Liability**			**Credit**
Date	*Account*	*Amount*	*Date*	*Account*	*Amount*
...	Bank/Purchases	21.50	...	Bank/Sales	45.80
...	Balance	24.30			
		45.80			45.80
			...	Balance	24.30

The VAT liability T account calculates the amount of VAT due to the revenue commissioners (€24.30) by subtracting the VAT on purchases (€21.50) from the VAT on sales (€45.80). This account will appear in the trial balance and represents the amount of VAT due to the revenue commissions at the date of the trial balance.

When the VAT is paid to the revenue commissioner this reduces the bank and also reduces the liability in the VAT Liability account. If the business paid VAT of €24.30 it would be recorded as follows:

Table 9.9 Journal Entry to Record the Payment of VAT

Date	**Account**	**Debit**	**Credit**
...	VAT liability	24.30	
...	Bank		24.30
Being payment of VAT			

Borrowings

When a company borrows from a bank this transaction must be recorded in the financial statements. When the company receives the loan it has more assets and more liabilities. For example, suppose a company borrows €50,000 from a bank at an interest rate of 6%. The interest is payable half yearly and the capital amount of the loan is repayable at the end of 10 years. This transaction would be recorded as follows

Table 9.5 Journal Entry to Record Borrowing from a Bank

Date	Account	Debit	Credit
...	Bank (BS)	50,000	
...	Loan (BS)		50,000
Being loan drawdown			

Table 9.6

Debit		Bank			Credit
Date	*Account*	*Amount*	*Date*	*Account*	*Amount*
...	Loan	50,000			

Debit		Loan			Credit
Date	*Account*	*Amount*	*Date*	*Account*	*Amount*
			...	Bank	50,000

The loan is a liability as it is owed back to the bank. Each half year the company has to pay interest on the loan. In this case this is €1,500 (50,000 x 6% x 6/12.) When the interest is paid the company will record the payment of interest as follows:

Table 9.7 Journal entry to record payment of interest

Date	Account	Debit	Credit
...	Interest on long term loan (IS)	1,500	
...	Bank (SOFP)		1,500

Interest is an expense and will appear in the income statement.

Chapter 9 Exercises

Exercise 9.1
Know-it-all Consultants

A recent graduate of UCD Quinn School sets up a consultancy company called Know-it-all Consultants. During the first year of business she enters into the following transactions.

1	The owner contributes €30,000 in capital to the company. She receives 30,000 ordinary shares of €1 each.
2	The owner signs a three year lease on premises. The rent is payable half yearly in advance. She pays €3,000 for the first half year.
3	Purchased office furniture for €1,000.
4	Purchased motor vehicle for €5,000.
5	Completed an assignment for a client. Client has agreed to pay €26,000.
6	Paid wages of €2,000.
7	Client from 5 above pays €6,000.
8	Paid office expenses of €2,000.
9	Depreciate the motor van over 5 years and the office furniture over 10 years. Use straight line depreciation with no residual value.
10	She finds an unpaid ESB bill for €500 in a drawer.

Record each of these transactions on the attached template. For example if you believe transaction 1 increases bank then put Dr. 30,000 in the bank row of the transaction 1 column.
Sum across each column.

In this way you should prepare Know-it-all Consultant's Income Statement for the first year of trading and a Statement of financial position at the end of the first year of trading. Make sure to record any year-end adjustments that are necessary (Hint – rent).

Statement of financial position of Know-it-all Consultants

	1	*2*	*3*	*4*	*5*	*6*	*7*	*8*	*9*	*10*	*11*	*Total*
Non-current assets												
Motor vehicles												
Accumulated depreciation on motor vehicles												
Office furniture												
Accumulated depreciation on office furniture												
Total non-current assets												
Current assets												
Receivables												
Bank												
Prepayments												
Total current assets												
Total assets												
Equity												
Equity share capital												
Retained income												
Total equity												
Current liabilities												
Accruals												
Total current liabilities												
Total equity and liabilities												

(Columns 1–11 under the heading *Transaction*.)

Income Statement of Know-it-all Consultants

	Transaction											
	1	*2*	*3*	*4*	*5*	*6*	*7*	*8*	*9*	*10*	*11*	***Total***
Revenues												
Less costs												
Rent												
Wages												
Office expenses												
Depreciation on motor van												
Depreciation on office furniture												
ESB												
Net profit												

Exercise 9.2 - Leopold Broom

Leopold Broom owns 100% of the share capital of Broom International Traders Ltd.

Broom International Traders Ltd.
Trial Balance as at 1 January 20X2. (Note: This is the opening trial balance)

	Debit	***Credit***
	€	€
Bank	11,000	
Premises	30,000	
Motor vehicle	12,000	
Accumulated depreciation on		
Premises		3,000
Motor vehicle		6,000
Inventory at 1.1.X2	11,000	
Receivables	25,000	
Payables		9,000
Bank loan (to be paid in full in 5 years time)		30,000
Share capital (1,000 ord. shares of €1 each)		1,000
Retained income		40,000
	89,000	89,000

During the year to 31.12.X2 the following transactions took place:

1. Sales of €250,000 were made. These sales were half on credit and half for cash. €100,000 was received from customers during the year

2. Purchases of €125,000 all on credit were made.

3. The following expenses were paid

Wages	€4,000
Light & heat	€3,000
Rent & rates	€2,000
Insurance	€4,000
Purchases	€100,000

4. The useful economic lives of the fixed assets are as follows

Premises	10 Years
Motor vehicle	4 Years

5. Leopold decided to set up a provision for bad debts of 5% of the year end receivables balance

6. Leopold discovered that a customer who owed €1,000 had gone into liquidation. He was told that he would receive nothing from this receivable.

7. Leopold discovers the following bills in a drawer

ESB for Nov. and Dec. X2	1,000
Insurance cover for the y/e 31.3.X3	4,000 (paid in note 3)

8. Leopold counted the inventory at 31.12.X2 and valued it at cost (€2,000)

REQUIRED

a) Prepare journal entries to record each of the transactions in 1-8 above.

b) Prepare the nominal ledger of L. Broom for the year ended 31.12.X2

c) Prepare an income statement for the year ended 31.12.X2

d) Prepare a statement of financial position as at 31.12.X2

e) Record the closing entries in the ledger of Leopold Broom.

NOTE: All statement of financial position accounts should be balanced
All income statement accounts should be transferred to a special income statement ledger account
The closing inventory should be entered into the ledger accounts

Chapter 10

The Financial Reporting Environment

Introduction

Financial accounting is affected by rules and regulations from many different sources. Company law provides a framework for financial reporting by companies while accounting standards provide guidance as to how financial statement should be prepared. This chapter surveys the main legislation and accounting standards governing financial statements. It does not cover less important legislation, stock exchange requirements or the requirements of more advanced accounting standards.

Financial Statements and Company Law

Every company registered in Ireland must prepare financial statements. This basis requirement is contained in the Companies Act, 1963 (CA 63).

Figure 10.1
The Requirement to Present Financial Statements

CA 63 S148 requires that every company present at the company's Annual General Meeting (AGM) an income statement and a statement of financial position.

These financial statements must show a 'True and Fair View.' This requirement is contained in the CA63 and also in the Companies (Amendment) Act, 1986 (CAA86)

Figure 10.2
The True and Fair Requirement

CA63 S149 and CAA86 S3 require that every such statement of financial position and income statement give ***a true and fair view*** of the state of affairs and of the profit or loss of the company for the financial year.

As well as presenting the financial statements at the Annual General Meeting (AGM) they must be filed with the Companies Registration Office (CRO). The financial statements are available to the general public for viewing from this office. The Companies Act, 1990 (CA90) S 202 imposes an obligation on the directors of the company to ensure that the company keeps proper books of account so that financial statements can be prepared at any reasonable time. CA63, CA86 and CA90 require specific disclosures in the accounts and to some extent, prescribe accounting methods for particular items.

A True and Fair View

A true and fair view is a legal concept. Ultimately, whether a set of financial statements give a 'True and Fair View' is a matter for the courts. It involves two main requirements being met. Firstly, the financial statements should meet all legal requirements. Secondly, accounting standards (IFRS) should have been followed when preparing the financial statements.

An Auditor is an independent accountant who provides the shareholders of a company with an audit opinion. The main part of the audit opinion is concerned with whether the financial statements give a true and fair view. An extract from CRH's Audit Report is given in Figure 10.3.

Figure 10.3
Extract from CRH's Audit Report 2005[36] (emphasis added)

Independent Auditors' Report
To the members of CRH public limited company
...
Opinion
In our opinion, the Group financial statements give **a true and fair view**, in accordance with IFRSs as adopted by the European Union, of the state of affairs of the Group as at 31st December 2005 and of its profit for the year then ended and have been properly prepared in accordance with the Companies Acts, 1963 to 2005 and Article 4 of the IAS Regulation.
...
We have obtained all the information and explanations we consider necessary for the purposes of our audit. In our opinion, proper books of account have been kept by the Company. The Company Statement of financial position is in agreement with the books of account.

[36] See www.crh.ie for the full audit report

Figure 10.3
Extract from CRH's Audit Report 2005[37] (emphasis added) (cont.)

In our opinion, the information given in the Directors' Report is consistent with the financial statements.

In our opinion, the Company Statement of financial position does not disclose a financial situation which under section 40(1) of the Companies (Amendment) Act, 1983 would require the convening of an extraordinary general meeting of the Company.

Ernst & Young
Registered Auditors

The Audit Report is addressed to the members of the company. This is because the auditor is engaged by the members at the AGM. The report states that in the auditors' opinion that the financial statements give a true and fair view. In general terms, this means that the shareholders rely on the auditors to make sure that the financial statements that have been prepared by the management of the company give a realistic view of the company's activities. The auditor is independent from the management of the company so this acts as a check on the management.

International Accounting Standards

In March 2001, the International Accounting Standards Committee (IASC) Foundation was formed as a not-for-profit corporation incorporated in the State of Delaware, US. The IASC took over from the International Accounting Standards Committee (IASC) which had been setting international standards for many years[38].

The IASC Foundation is the parent entity of the International Accounting Standards Board (IASB), an independent accounting standard-setter based in London, UK. The objectives of the IASC foundation are given in Figure 10.4.

[37] See www.crh.ie for the full audit report
[38] http://www.iasb.org/about/history.asp

Figure 10.4
Extract from the IASC Constitution

The objectives of the IASC Foundation are:

(a) to develop, in the public interest, a single set of high quality, understandable and enforceable global accounting standards that require high quality, transparent and comparable information in financial statements and other financial reporting to help participants in the world's capital markets and other users make economic decisions;
(b) to promote the use and rigorous application of those standards; and
(c) in fulfilling the objectives associated with (a) and (b), to take account of, as appropriate, the special needs of small and medium-sized entities and emerging economies; and
(d) to bring about convergence of national accounting standards and International Accounting Standards and International Financial Reporting Standards to high quality solutions.

The International Accounting Standards Board (IASB) actually issues the accounting standards. The IASB issues discussion papers on controversial areas in accounting, Exposure Drafts (ED) that set out proposed standards and International Accounting Standards (IAS) that are the final standards that must be apply when preparing financial statements. From January 2005 the EU has require the use of International Financial Reporting Standards for all **listed** (on a stock exchange) companies. This will mean that it will be easier to compare accounts from different EU countries.

Accounting Standards in Practice

Accounting standards have three main effects on financial statements. Firstly, they force companies to state their accounting policies clearly. Accounting policies are the ways in which companies prepare their financial statements. In some cases there can be a number of ways in which an accounting number like depreciation can be calculated. In is very important that the users of financial statements are able to see how the financial statements have been prepared. Figure 10.4 shows the property, plant and equipment note from CRH's annual report in 2005. This note gives the reader an insight into how depreciation is calculated in CRH's financial statements.

Figure 10.4
Property, Plant and Equipment Note from CRH's Financial Statements 2005

With the exception of the one-time revaluation of land and buildings noted below, items of property, plant and equipment are stated at historical cost less any accumulated depreciation and any accumulated impairments.

Depreciation and depletion
Depreciation is calculated to write off the book value of each item of property, plant and equipment over its useful economic life on a straight-line basis at the following rates:

Land and buildings:	The book value of mineral-bearing land, less an estimate of its residual value, is depleted over the period of the mineral extraction in the proportion which production for the year bears to the latest estimates of mineral reserves. Land other than mineral-bearing land is not depreciated. In general, buildings are depreciated at 2.5% p.a.
Plant and machinery:	These are depreciated at rates ranging from 3.3% p.a. to 20% p.a. depending on the type of asset.
Transport:	In general, transport equipment is depreciated at 20% p.a.

Certain items of property, plant and equipment that had been revalued to fair value prior to the date of transition to IFRS (1st January 2004) are measured on the basis of deemed cost, being the revalued amount as at the date the revaluation was performed.

The residual values and useful lives of property, plant and equipment are reviewed, and adjusted if appropriate, at each statement of financial position date.

Secondly, accounting standards only allow the use of some accounting techniques. For example, in the past some companies argued that buildings should not be depreciated while other companies did charge depreciation on buildings. Accounting standards now state that buildings must be depreciated leading to greater comparability between the financial statements of different companies.

Thirdly, accounting standards force companies to disclose information that they might not otherwise. For example, some large companies have various different business units or segments. Accounting standards require companies to provide a note showing the profit and assets of the company broken down by business unit. This provides useful information to investors who want to access the performance of each business unit.

Summary

Company law requires companies to prepare financial statements and present them to their shareholders. These financial statements must show a true and fair view. Accounting standards set out the accounting policies that are acceptable and determine the information that must be disclosed in financial statements.

Chapter 11

The Presentation of Financial Statements

Introduction

The presentation of financial statement is determined by accounting standards and company law. Company law requires the disclosure of particular items while accounting standards determine the items to be disclosed, their order, and their classification. In this chapter the basic layout of the income statement and the statement of financial position will be examined. The effect of legislation, stock exchange requirements and many accounting standards in determining the content and layout of financial statements is beyond the scope of this book.

The Structure of Financial Statements

IAS 1 *Presentation of financial statements* is the primary accounting standard concerned with the content and layout of financial statements. Figure 11.1 gives the definition of a complete set of financial statements from IAS 1. Requirement (b) from Figure 11.1 is for a statement of comprehensive income. This is an expanded version of the income statement[39]. Requirement (c) is for a statement of changes in equity where dividends and other equity changes are recorded. Requirement (d) is for a statement of cash flows which will be dealt with in Chapter 13 of this book. Requirement (f) is for a set of notes to accompany the financial statements.

[39] The income statement is one part of the statement of comprehensive income. IAS 1 does allow the continued use of the 'income statement' title where the statement of comprehensive income is split into two parts. This is the treatment that is adopted in this book.

Figure 11.1[40]
IAS 1 Contents of a complete set of financial statements

10 A complete set of financial statements comprises:
(a) a statement of financial position as at the end of the period;
(b) a statement of comprehensive income for the period;
(c) a statement of changes in equity for the period;
(d) a statement of cash flows for the period;
(e) notes, comprising a summary of significant accounting policies and other explanatory information; and
...

The Statement of Financial Position

The statement of financial position shows the assets, liabilities and equity of the business entity at the end of the reporting period. Assets and liabilities must be split into current and non-current (see Figures 7.1 & 9.1). Table 11.1 shows how the statement of financial position is organised[41]. The balance sheet usually begins with non-current assets and then gives current assets. Subtotals are given after each category of item. The statement of financial position is totalled 'Total assets' on the assets side. The other part of the balance sheet gives the equity items, non-current liabilities and current liabilities. The statement of financial position is totalled 'Total equity and liabilities' on the equity and liabilities side.

[40] IASC, 2008, IAS 1 Presentation of financial statements (annual periods beginning on or after 1 January 2009 with earlier adoption permitted)
[41] The statement of financial position can be presented in different ways under IAS 1. The method used by most firms (given in Table 11.1) is the one used in this book.

Table 11.1 Statement of Financial Position at 31st December 2005

	€'000
ASSETS	
Non-current assets	
Property, plant and equipment	X
Total non-current assets	X
Current assets	
Inventories	X
Receivables	X
Cash and cash equivalents	X
Total current assets	X
Total assets	X
EQUITY	
Equity share capital	X
Share premium	X
Retained income	X
Total equity	X
LIABILITIES	
Non-current liabilities	
Interest-bearing loans and borrowings	X
Current liabilities	
Payables	X
Tax	X
Accruals	X
Total current liabilities	X
Total liabilities	X
Total equity and liabilities	X

The Income Statement

The income statement shows the income and expenditure of the business entity for the reporting period. Table 11.2 shows the organisation of the income statement. It begins with sales revenue from which the cost of sales is subtracted to give gross profit. Distribution costs, administration expenses and any other operating expenses are the deducted. Any other operating income is then added back. This gives operating profit. Finance costs are then deducted and finance income is added back. This gives profit before taxation. The taxation charge for the year is then deducted to give profit for the financial year.

Table 11.2 Income Statement for the year ended 31st December 2005

	€'000
Revenue	X
Cost of sales	X
Gross profit	X
Distribution costs	X
Administration expenses	X
Other operating expenses	X
Other operating income	X
Operating profit	X
Finance costs	X
Finance revenue	X
Profit before tax	X
Income tax expense	X
Profit for the financial year	X

Company Law Disclosure Requirements

Company law requires the disclosure of a number of specific items that are given in Figure 11.2. These disclosures are designed to provide more information for the owners of the business entity. For example, the owners are informed by this note about the director's remuneration.

Figure 11.2
Company law requires the following items to be disclosed

(a) Total depreciation for the period;
(b) Staff costs for the period;
(c) The audit fee;
(d) Directors' fees; and
(e) Directors' salaries (including pension contribution and bonuses).

Note: Company law requires many more disclosures that are beyond the scope of this book

Classification of expenses

The firm's expenditure must be classified into the various categories that are provided in the income statement. Figure 11.3 gives some guidance as to how expenditure should be classified. Cost of sales should include all expenses that can be directly related to making or buying-in the goods that the company sells. Administration expenses should include all expenses concerned with administering the business. Distribution costs should include all marketing, selling and distribution expenses.

Figure 11.3
Classification of expenditure

Distribution costs includes warehouse costs, all selling and distribution costs, motor expenses (if relating to sales), bad debts and increases in the bad debt provision, depreciation on delivery vehicles and warehouse building and salaries for sales and warehouse employees.

Administration expenses includes light and heat, insurance, office salaries, directors' expenses and salaries, directors' motor expenses (excluding sales director or production director), bank charges, stationary and postage, audit fee and depreciation on fixtures and fittings and office buildings and on directors' and managers' cars.

Cost of sales includes all factory expenses such as factory wages, factory insurance, patent costs relating to production, depreciation on plant and machinery and factory building.

Summary

In this chapter the basic requirements of company law and accounting standards for the presentation of financial statement were examined. The statement of financial position and the income statement must be presented. The layout and content of these financial statements is mainly determined by IAS 1.

Chapter 12

The Preparation of Financial Statements – Part II

Introduction

Financial statements are usually composed of a statement of financial position, an income statement, a statement of cash flows and notes. This chapter brings together all of the material in earlier chapters and shows how financial statements are prepared. In this chapter, an income statement and statement of financial position together with basic notes will be prepared from a trial balance. These financial statements will be formatted according to the rules contained in IAS 1.

Preparation of Financial Statements

Financial statements are usually prepared using the process described in Figure 12.1.

Figure 12.1
The Steps in Preparing Financial Statements

1. The transactions for the financial period are expressed as journal entries and entered into T accounts.
2. A trial balance is extracted from the completed T accounts.
3. Information about any required adjustments is gathered. These adjustments may include items such as:
   - Depreciation of non-current assets:
   - Impairment of receivables;
   - Increasing or decreasing allowances for credit losses;
   - Recording accruals or prepayments;
   - Providing for the corporation tax charge;
   - Recording the closing inventory.
4. The financial statements are preparing using the trial balance and the information about the adjustments required.

Figure 12.1 (cont.)

5. When the financial statements are finalised the adjustments are recorded as journal entries and in the T accounts.
6. All of the T accounts relating to the income statement are transferred to the retained income account thereby setting those accounts to zero.
7. The closing inventory is transferred to the inventory account.
8. The T accounts are closed for the financial year. Only statement of financial position T accounts should have a balance. An opening trial balance can now be prepared for next year.

At the end of each financial period a trial balance is prepared (Figure 12.1 step 2). This trial balance reflects all of the basic transactions that have been recorded during the financial period. It should reflect all of the sales, purchases, expenses, receipts and payments that have occurred during the period. The accountant must also search for any additional information that may be required to finalise the financial statements. This information usually concerns the depreciation charge on non-current assets, changes in the allowance for credit losses, accruals and prepayments and the closing inventory (Figure 12.1 Step 3). These items are known collectively as 'period-end adjustments.' Using the trial balance and the additional information about period-end adjustments the accountant prepares the financial statements. When the financial statements have been finalised the accountant records all of these adjustments in T accounts and prepares a closing trial balance.

The process of preparing financial statements will be illustrated using the information in Tables 12.1 and 12.4. Table 12.1 contains the trial balance for Merrion plc at the end of the 20x5 financial year. Table 12.4 contains the additional information collected about potential period-end adjustments.

Table 12.1 Merrion plc's Trial Balance as at 31 December 20x5

Item		Dr. €'000	Cr. €'000
1	Allowance for credit losses		50
2	Equity share capital (ordinary shares €2.00 each)		400
3	Share premium		1,300
4	Receivables and payables	3,400	2,100
5	Land (cost)	1,700	
6	Motor vehicles at cost	120	
7	Motor vehicles accumulated depreciation		40
8	Fixtures and fittings at cost	640	
9	Fixtures and fittings accumulated depreciation		210
10	Buildings at cost	3,200	
11	Buildings accumulated depreciation		312
12	Bank	183	
13	Administration expenses	1,900	
14	Audit fee	130	
15	Directors' fees	40	
16	Directors' salaries	890	
17	Inventory	2,090	
18	Advertising	418	
19	Purchases and sales	10,900	20,200
20	Delivery expenses	1,200	
21	Warehouse salaries	260	
22	Office salaries	490	
23	Retained income 1 January 20x5		1,949
24	7% Term loan		1,000
		27,561	27,561

Table 12.1 contains the trial balance of Merrion plc at the end of 20x5. The trial balance reflects all of the transactions that were recorded during 20x5. For example, the advertising line item has €418,000 on the debit side of the trial balance. This means that at some point during the financial year entries were recorded that created an expense of €418,000 for advertising. For example, the company may have paid a local newspaper €2,000 for advertising services. This would have been recorded as follows:

Table 12.2 Journal Entry to Advertising Expense

Date	Account	Debit	Credit
...	Advertising	2,000	
...	Bank		2,000

Being advertising expense paid by cash.

The trial balance does not show the individual transactions that were recorded during the period but it does show the overall result of recorded all of these transactions. Table 12.3 shows that items in the trial balance are classified in the same way as the balances on T accounts (see Table 4.5). Debit balances are either an asset or an expense and credit items are either a liability, an equity item or a revenue item.

Table 12.3 Classification of Trial Balance Items

Debit	Credit
An asset	A liability or equity item
or	Or
An expense or a loss	A revenue or a gain

For example the equity share capital (item 2 in Table 12.1) is an equity item and is on the credit side while land (item 5 in Table 12.1) is a non-current asset and is on the debit side.

Table 12.4 shows the additional information that has been collected by the accountant about Merrion plc. This information has not been incorporated into the trial balance but must be reflected in the financial statements.

Table 12.4 Additional Information Available About Merrion plc at 31 December 20x5

1 The useful lives of the non-current assets are as follows: -

Buildings	40 years
Fixtures and fittings	10 years
Motor vehicles	4 years

Depreciation is to be provided using the straight-line basis and assuming a zero residual value. None of the assets have reached the end of their useful lives. The motor vehicles are used by delivery staff. The buildings are used 80% as a warehouse and 20% as an office. Fixtures and fittings are office equipment.

2 After a review of the receivables it is decided to record an impairment of €20,000 against the account of a large customer. An allowance for credit losses of €169,000 is required for the remaining receivables.

3 The 7% term loan has to be repaid on 31 December, 20y9. It was received on 1 January, 20x3.

4 It is proposed to pay a final dividend of €1.60 per share in respect of the year to 31 December, 20x5. No accounting entries have been made with regard to this dividend.

5 Inventory at the lower of cost or net realisable value on 31 December, 20x5 is €2,980,000.

6 Corporation tax for the year ended 31 December, 20x5 has been estimated at €502,000.

The financial statements will be prepared using the trial balance (Table 12.2) and the additional information (Table 12.4). When preparing financial statements the following procedure can be useful

Figure 12.2
Preparing Financial Statements

1. Read through the trial balance noting where each item belongs in the financial statements (e.g. a non-current asset or an administration expense).
2. Read through the additional information and decide how these items will affect the financial statements.
3. Calculate the expense categories in the income statement (cost of goods sold, administration expenses, distribution expenses, other operation costs, and other operation income)
4. Prepare the income statement.
5. Prepare the statutory disclosures required.
6. Prepare the property, plant and equipment note to the statement of financial position.
7. Prepare the statement of financial position.

Step 1
Read through the trial balance noting where each item belongs in the financial statements (e.g. a non-current asset or an administration expense).

Table 12.5 Merrion plc's Trial Balance as at 31 December 20x5

Item		**Dr. €'000**	**Cr. €'000**	**Item type**
1	Allowance for credit losses		50	Subtracted from receivables in the statement of financial position
2	Equity share capital (ordinary shares €2.00 each)		400	Equity section of the statement of financial position
3	Share premium		1,300	Equity section of the statement of financial position
4	Receivables and payables	3,400	2,100	Receivables (Dr.) are a current asset and payables (Cr.) are a current liability
5	Land (cost)	1,700		A non-current asset

Table 12.5 (cont.)

6	Motor vehicles at cost	120		A non-current asset
7	Motor vehicles accumulated depreciation		40	Subtracted from the cost of motor vehicles in the non-current asset section of the Statement of financial position
8	Fixtures and fittings at cost	640		A non-current asset
9	Fixtures and fittings accumulated depreciation		210	Subtracted from the cost of fixtures and fittings in the non-current asset section of the Statement of financial position
10	Buildings at cost	3,200		A non-current asset
11	Buildings accumulated depreciation		312	Subtracted from the cost of buildings in the non-current asset section of the Statement of financial position
12	Bank	183		A current asset
13	Administration expenses	1,900		An administration expense
14	Audit fee	130		An administration expense
15	Directors' fees	40		An administration expense
16	Directors' salaries	890		An administration expense
17	Inventory	2,090		A current asset
18	Advertising	418		An administration expense
19	Purchases and sales	10,900	20,200	Sales are shown as revenue in the income statement. Purchases form part of the cost of sales calculation
20	Delivery expenses	1,200		A distribution expense

Table 12.5 (cont.)

21	Warehouse salaries	260		A distribution expense
22	Office salaries	490		An administration expense
23	Retained income 1 January 20x5		1,949	Equity section of the statement of financial position
24	7% Term loan		1,000	Non-current liabilities section of the statement of financial position
		27,561	27,561	

Step 2
Read through the additional information and decide how these items will affect the financial statements

The depreciation note (Table 12.4 (1)) indicates the useful lives that are to be used for each class of non-current asset. The note states that the straight line method of depreciation is to be used. This means that the costs of the non-current assets given in the trial balance should be divided by their useful lives to give the depreciation charge for this year. Table 12.6 shows the calculation of the annual depreciation charge for each of the non-current asset classes using straight line depreciation. For each class of non-current asset the depreciable amount is divided by the useful life of the assets[42].

[42] In this case, the depreciable amount is equal to the cost of the assets in the trial balance because (a) there were no acquisitions or disposals of assets during the year; (b) none of the assets had reached the end of their useful lives (stated in Table 12.5) and (c) all of the assets had a zero residual value.

Table 12.6 Calculation of the Depreciation Charges

	20x5
Depreciable amount of buildings(cost of the asset – item 10 in Table 12.1)	€3,200,000
÷ useful life of buildings (from Table 12.6)	40 years
Depreciation charge on buildings	€80,000
To be divided between the following cost categories	
Distribution (warehouse) 80%	€64,000
Administration (office) 20%	€16,000
Depreciable amount of motor vehicles (cost of the asset – item 6 in Table 12.1)	€120,000
÷ useful life of motor vehicles (from Table 12.6)	4 years
Depreciation charge on motor vehicles	€30,000
Depreciable amount of fixtures and fittings (cost of the asset – item 8 in Table 12.1)	€640,000
÷ useful life of fixtures and fittings (from Table 12.6)	10 years
Depreciation charge on fixtures and fittings	€64,000

These depreciation charges will need to be charged as an expense in the income statement and added to the accumulated depreciation balances in the statement of financial position.

The doubtful receivables (Table 12.4 (2)) note states that the allowance for credit losses is to be €169,000 and that receivables are to be impaired by €20,000. The receivables and the charge to the income statement for impairments must be calculated.

Table 12.7 Calculation of Increase in Allowance for Credit Losses

	€
New allowance for credit losses	169,000
Old allowance for credit losses	50,000
Increase in allowance	119,000

Table 12.8 Journal Entry to Record the Increase in the Allowance for Credit Losses

Date	Account	Debit	Credit
...	Increase in allowance for credit losses (IS)	119,000	
...	Allowance for credit losses		119,000

Table 12.9 Calculation of Receivables in Merrion's Statement of Financial Position

	€
Receivables	3,400,000
Less Impairment	(20,000)
	3,380,000
Less Allowance for credit losses	169,000
Net receivables	3,211,000

The note in Table 12.4 (3) indicates that interest must be paid on the long term loans at the rate of 7%. The long term loans amount to €1,000,000 (item 24 from Table 12.1). The interest on this loan will amount to €70,000 (€1,000,000 x 7%). This interest must be accrued as it does not appear in the trial balance as an expense. We record the accrual by including the interest as an expense in the income statement and recording a current liability for interest in the statement of financial position. The journal entry to record the accrual is as follows:

Table 12.10 Calculation of Loan Interest

Amount of long term loan (item 24 from Table 12.1)	€1,000,000
Interest rate (given in Table 12.12)	7%
Annual interest charge	€70,000

Table 12.11 Journal Entry to Record Accrued Interest

Date	Account	Debit	Credit
...	Interest expense (IS)	70,000	
...	Interest accrued (SOFP)		70,000

Table 12.4 (4) indicates that the company intends to pay a dividend after the end of the accounting period. Under IFRS rules 'proposed dividends' are now recorded in the financial statements until they are paid so there is no need to adjust the financial statements for this transaction.

The closing inventory figure (Table 12.4 (5)) of €2,980,000 is used in two places in the financial statements. It will be used in the cost of sales calculation as the closing inventory and entered as a current asset in the statement of financial position.

Information about corporation tax is given in Table 12.4 (6). The amount of tax due for the accounting period is €502,000. This amount will be entered as an expense in the income statement. If there had been a payment of preliminary corporation tax it would have appeared on the trial balance as a debit balance. In this case, it does not appear that there was a payment of corporation tax so the full amount of corporation tax must also be recorded as a current liability. The entry to record corporation tax is given in Table 12.12

Table 12.12 Journal Entry to Record Corporation Tax

Date	Account	Debit	Credit
...	Corporation tax expense (IS)	502,000	
...	Corporation tax due (SOFP)		502,000

Step 3
Calculate the expense categories in the income statement (cost of sales, administration expenses, distribution expenses, other operation costs and other operation income)

We calculate the figures that will appear under the various headings in the income statement using the information in the trial balance (Table 12.1) and any information about expenses like depreciation and bad debts that is contained in the additional information (Table 12.4)

Table 12.13 Workings to Calculate the Figures for Cost of Sales, Administration Expenses and Distribution Expenses

Cost of Sales	**€'000**
Opening inventory (item 17 from Table 12.1)	2,090
Purchases (item 19 from Table 12.1)	10,900
Closing inventory (item 5 from table 12.4)	(2,980)
Cost of sales	10,010

Administration expenses	**€'000**
Administration expenses (item 13 from table 12.1)	1,900
Audit fee (item 14 from table 12.1)	130
Directors' fees (item 15 from table 12.1)	40
Directors' salaries (item 16 from table 12.1)	890
Office salaries (item 22 from table 12.1)	490
Depreciation on office buildings (calculated in Table 12.6)	16
Depreciation on fixtures and fittings (calculated in Table 12.6)	64
Administration expenses	3,530

Distribution costs	**€'000**
Impairment of receivables (from Table 12.4 item 2)	20
Allowance for credit losses (calculated in Table 12.7)	119
Delivery expenses (item 20 from Table 12.1)	1,200
Advertising (item 18 from Table 12.1)	418
Warehouse salaries (item 21 from Table 12.1)	260
Depreciation on motor vehicles (calculated in Table 12.6)	30
Depreciation on warehouse building (calculated in Table 12.6)	64
Distribution costs	2,111

Step 4
Prepare the income statement.

The income statement can now be prepared using the information in Table 12.14 and the trial balance (Table 12.1).

Table 12.14 Merrion plc Income Statement for the year ended 31.12.2005

	Source	**€'000**
Revenue	Item 19 Table 12.1	20,200
Cost of sales	Table 12.13	(10,010)
Gross profit		10,190
Distribution costs	Table 12.13	(2,111)
Administration expenses	Table 12.13	(3,530)
Other operating expenses		
Other operating income		
Operating profit		4,549
Finance costs	Table 12.10	(70)
Finance revenue		
Profit before tax		4,479
Income tax expense	Item 6 Table 12.4	(502)
Profit for the financial year		3,977

Step 5
Prepare the statutory disclosures required.

As well as preparing the income statement we also prepare a note containing various items required by the companies act. This note (Table 12.16) usually contains information on audit fees, directors' fees, directors' salaries, salaries and wages and depreciation.

Table 12.15 Merrion plc Calculation of Total Depreciation

	€'000
Depreciation charge on buildings (Table 12.6)	80
Depreciation charge on motor vehicles (Table 12.6)	30
Depreciation charge on fixtures and fittings (Table 12.6)	64
	174

Table 12.16 Merrion plc 'Operating profit' note for the year ended 31.12.2005

Operating profit has been arrived at after charging the following amounts:	**Source**	**€'000**
Audit fee	Item 14 Table 12.1	130
Directors' fees	Item 15 Table 12.1	40
Directors' salaries	Item 16 Table 12.1	890
Salaries and wages	Items 21,22 Table 12.1	750
Depreciation	(Table 12.15)	174

Step 6
Prepare the property, plant and equipment note to the statement of financial position.

The property, plant and equipment note to the statement of financial position calculates the Net Book Value of Merrion plc's non current assets at the end of the financial year. The note is split horizontally into 3 sections. The first section traces the cost of the assets from the start of the year to the end of the year. The second section traces accumulated depreciation from the start of the year to the end of the year. The third section shows Net Book Value (NBV) which is cost less accumulated depreciation at the end of the financial year. Each column in the table shows the cost, accumulated depreciation and NBV of a category of non-current assets.

The figures for both cost and accumulated depreciation for the various categories of non-current assets at the start of the year are taken from the trial balance (Table 12.1). The figures for depreciation are taken from Table 12.6.

Table 12.17 Merrion plc Note on Property, Plant and Equipment

	Land	Buildings	Motor	Fixtures and Fittings	Total
Cost	**€'000**	**€'000**	**€'000**	**€'000**	**€'000**
at 1/1/20x6 (items 5,6,8 &10 from Table 12.1)	1,700	3,200	120	640	5,660
Additions	-	-	-	-	-
Disposals	-	-	-	-	-
at 31/12/20x6	1,700	3,200	120	640	5,660
Accumulated depreciation					
at 1/1/20x6 (items 7,9,11 from Table 12.1)	0	312	40	210	562
Charge (from Table 12.6)	-	80	30	64	-
	-	-	-	-	-
at 31/12/20x6	0	392	70	274	736
Net Book Value at 31/12/20x6	1,700	2,808	50	366	4,924

Step 7
Prepare the statement of financial position.

The statement of financial position can now be prepared. The figure for non-current assets is the NBV of the total of the NBVs of the categories of non-current assets in Table 12.17.

Table 12.18 Merrion plc Calculation of Retained Income as at 31st December 20x5

	€'000
Retained income as at 1 January 20x5 (item 23 table 12.1)	1,949
Add profit for the financial year (Table 12.14)	3,977
Less dividends paid	-
	5,926

Table 12.19 Merrion plc Statement of financial position of Merrion plc as at 31st December 2005

	Source	€'000
ASSETS		
Non-current assets		
Property, plant and equipment	Table 12.17	4,924
		4,924
Current assets		
Inventories	Item 5 Table 12.4	2,980
Receivables	Table 12.9	3,211
Cash and cash equivalents	Item 12 from Table 12.1	183
Total current assets		6,374
Total assets		11,298
EQUITY		
Equity share capital	Item 2 Table 12.1	400
Share premium	Item 3 Table 12.1	1,300
Retained income	Table 12.18	5,926
Total equity		7,626
LIABILITIES		
Non-current liabilities		
Interest-bearing loans and borrowings	Item 24 Table 12.1	1,000
Current liabilities		
Payables	Item 4 Table 12.1	2,100
Tax	Item 6 Table 12.2	502
Accruals	Table 12.10	70
Total current liabilities		2,672
Total liabilities		3,672
Total equity and liabilities		11,298

Conclusion

In this chapter we have taken the trial balance and some additional information about the company and turned this information into an income statement and a statement of financial position. Using this method the outputs of the bookkeeping system can be transformed into information useful to the users of financial statements.

Chapter 12 Exercises

Exercise 12.1

The following income statement has been prepared for **Lotti plc** for the year ended 31 March 20x6.

	€'000	**€'000**
Sales		2,500
Less: Sales Returns		(200)
		2,300
Opening Inventory	500	
Purchases	1,000	
Delivery Expenses	100	
Sales Director's Salary	200	
Closing Inventory	(100)	(1,700)
Gross Profit		600
Dividends Received		100
Rent Received		50
		750
Expenses		
Audit Fee	5	
Factory Wages	100	
Warehouse Expenses	10	
Depreciation – Vehicles	28	
- Plant	10	
- Fittings & Fixtures	29	
Wages and Salaries – Administration	180	
- Sales	124	
Directors' Fees	25	
Selling Expenses	80	
Managing Director's Salary	50	
Interest (loan repayable 20x9)	12	
Taxation	30	
Light and Heat	18	
Stationery	6	(707)
Net Profit		43
Dividends paid		(12)
Retained profit		31
Retained Earnings 1 April 20x5		180
Retained Earnings 31 March 20x6		211

Requirement: Prepare the income statement of Lotti plc for the year ended 31 March 20x6 under IFRS.

Exercise 12.2

The following is the Trial Balance of **Mame plc,** as at 31 December, 20x6.

	€ **Debit**	€ **Credit**
Authorised and issued share capital (ordinary shares of €1 each, fully paid)		500,000
Land at cost	1,200,000	
Office buildings, at cost	330,000	
Factory, at cost	660,000	
Motor vehicles, at cost	230,500	
Accumulated depreciation on office buildings to 31 December, 20x5		55,000
Accumulated depreciation on motor vehicles to 31 December, 20x5		54,500
Accumulated depreciation on factory to 31 December, 20x5		242,000
Administration costs	102,000	
Selling expenses	59,000	
Packing costs	11,000	
Factory salaries and wages	423,000	
Administration salaries and wages	120,000	
Sales salaries and wages	53,000	
Impairment of receivables	11,800	
Audit fee	3,200	
Office equipment repairs and maintenance	900	
Inventory, 31 December, 20x5	1,300,000	
Purchases	12,600,000	
Sales		14,560,000
Directors' salaries	210,000	
Directors' fees	20,000	
Long term loans (interest rate 12%)		150,000
Interest on long term loans	9,000	
Bank	111,000	
Receivables and payables	782,000	467,000
Ordinary dividend (net) paid 30 June, 20x6.	230,000	
Retained income		2,437,900
	18,466,400	18,466,400

You ascertain the following:

(1) The useful lives of the fixed assets are as follows:-

Office buildings	30 years
Factory	30 years
Motor vehicles	4 years

Depreciation is to be provided using the straight line basis and assuming a zero residual value. None of the assets have reached the end of their useful lives. The motor vehicles are used by sales staff.

(2) After a review of the receivables it is decided to record an impairment of €3,000 due to the liquidation of a customer. An allowance for credit losses of €38,950 is to be established for the remaining receivables.

(3) The 12% long term loan has to be repaid on 31 December, 2010. The interest is paid half yearly.

(4) It is proposed to pay a final dividend of 5c per share in respect of the year to 31 December, 20x6. No accounting entries have been made with regard to this dividend.

(5) Inventory at the lower of cost or net realisable value on 31 December, 20x6 is €1,210,000.

(6) Corporation tax for the year ended 31 December, 20x6 has been estimated at €190,500.

Required:

You are required to prepare:

(a) An income statement for the year ended 31 December, 20x6.
(b) The 'Operating profit is stated after charging/(crediting)' note.
(c) A statement of financial position as at 31 December, 20x6.
(d) The 'Property, plant and equipment' note.

Chapter 13

The Statement of Cash Flows

Introduction

Financial statements are usually composed of a statement of financial position, an income statement and a statement of cash flows. The statement of cash flows shows how the business has acquired cash during the year and how it has spent that cash. It differs from the income statement because it focuses on the inflows and outflows of cash and does not use the accruals concept.

Profits and Cash Flows

The income statement is prepared under the accruals concept. This means that transactions are recorded when they occur rather than when they are paid or received in cash. For example, a business will record a sale when the goods are delivered to a customer's premises rather than when the customer pays for those goods. However, only sales revenues that have actually been received will appear in the statement of cash flows. The statement of cash flows reports the amounts of cash that have been received and paid and ignores transactions that have not yet had a cash effect. This means that the income statement and the statement of cash flows can show very different pictures of the firm's position. For example, the income statement of ABC ltd. (Table 13.2) shows a healthy profit of €10,000 but the amount of cash on the statement of financial position (table 13.1) has declined by €5,000.

Table 13.1 Statement of financial position of ABC Ltd. at 31 December

ASSETS	**2006**	**2005**
	€'000	**€'000**
Cash	2	7
Receivables	25	10
	27	17
EQUITY		
Ordinary Share Capital (€1 shares)	2	2
Retained profits	25	15
	27	17

Income Statement of ABC Ltd. for year ended 31/12/06 (Extract)

	€'000
Revenue	50
Expenses (all paid in cash)	(40)
Profit for the financial year	10

How can the statement of financial position show that the amount of cash has declined by €5,000 but the income statements statement show a profit of €10,000? The answer is that the income statement is showing the outcome of all the transactions that have occurred. Some of these transactions may have not yet turned into 'money in the bank.' The income statement shows sales revenue of €50,000. The receivables figures in the statement of financial position shows that customers owed the business €10,000 at the end of 2005 and €25,000 at the end of 2006. This means that sales of €15,000 must have been made during the year that were not paid for until after the end of 2006. Using this information a simple statement of cash flows can be prepared.

Table 13.2 Simplified Statement of cash flows of ABC Ltd. for year ended 31/12/06

	€'000
Bank balance at the start of the year	7
Add: cash received from customers (10 + 50 -25)	35
Less: cash paid for expenses	(40)
Bank balance at the end of the year	2

There are other items that can cause similar differences between the income statement and the statement of cash flows. If a business purchases non-current assets during the year this will reduce the bank balance but will only reduce the profit by the amount of depreciation on the asset.

The Indirect Method

A statement of cash flows could be prepared by looking back at all the entries in the businesses bank account and summarizing them. However, statements of cash flows are usually prepared using a 'short cut'. This indirect method allows the preparation of the statement of cash flows using the income statement and statement of financial position that have already been prepared. The method works by starting with the accounting equation and then breaking it down into its constituent parts. The expanded accounting equation is then written in changes rather than in absolute amounts. Figure 13.1 shows how this method can produce a formula for 'Change in cash' which is what we need to explain in the statement of cash flows.

Figure 13.1
Calculating Cash Flows from the Accounting Equation

Assets - Liabilities = Equity

Or

(Other assets + Cash) - Liabilities = Issued Share Capital + Retained Income

Or

Change in Other Assets + Change in Cash - Change in Liabilities
= Change in Issued Share capital + Change in Retained Income

Or

Change in Cash = (Change in Retained Income - Change in Other Assets)
+ Change in Liabilities + Change in Issued Share Capital

This method will be illustrated using an example. Table 13.3 gives the statements of financial position for 2005 and 2006 and the income statement for 2006 of Branch Ltd.

Table 13.3
Branch Ltd. Statement of financial position as at 31 December

	2006	2005
	€'000	€'000
Non-current assets	120	120
Inventory	60	50
Receivables	65	70
Cash	53	21
	298	261
Share capital	150	150
Retained income	43	21
Payables	90	80
Long term loan	15	10
	298	261

Branch Ltd. Income Statement for the year ended 31 December 2006

	€'000
Operating profit	22
Profit for the financial year	22

The statement of cash flows can be prepared using the formulas given in Figure 13.1. Table 13.4 demonstrates how the changes in other figures in the statement of financial position can be used to explain the change in cash.

Table 13.4
Change in Cash=
(Change in Retained Earnings - Change in Other Assets)
+ Change in Liabilities + Change in Issued Share Capital

		€'000	
Change in cash (53-21)		32	This figure is what we are trying to explain
=			
Change in Retained Income (43-21)		22	We could also call this profit
- Change in Other Assets			
Receivables (65-70)	-5		
Inventory (60-50)	10	-5	The net change in other assets is 5. We need to take that away (note the minus before change in other assets in the equation)
+ Change in liabilities			
Payables (90-80)		10	
Long term loan (15-10)		5	
+ Change in issued share capital		0	
		32	Adding up the other side of the equation we get our change in cash back again

The statement in Table 13.4 can then be re-arranged into an IAS 7 statement of cash flows given below in Table 13.5.

Table 13.5
Branch Ltd.
Statement of cash flows for the year ended 31.12.2006 under IAS7

	€'000
Operating activities	
Operating profit	22
Add Depreciation charges	0
Change in receivables	5
Change in inventory	-10
Change in payables	10
Interest paid	0
Tax paid	0
Operating cash flow	**27**
Investing activities	
Payments to acquire non-current assets	0
Financing Activities	
Increase in long term debt	5
Increase/(Decrease) in cash	32

This procedure can be summarized in the steps given in Figure 13.2.

Figure 13.2
How to Prepare a Statement of cash flows

1) Take Profit before Interest and Tax (usually called 'profit before finance costs')
2) Add back depreciation, loss on sale of assets
3) Subtract profit on sale of asset
4) Show inflows and outflows from current assets and liabilities
   Increase in receivables/inventory = outflow (subtract)
   Increase in payables = inflow (add)
5) Work out interest ***paid.*** (You may have to work this out using interest due on the statements of financial position and interest charged in the income statement)
6) Work out tax ***paid.*** (You may have to work this out using tax due on the statements of financial position and tax charged in the income statement)

Figure 13.2 (cont.)

7) This gives cash inflow/outflow from operations
8) Work out additions/disposals of non-current assets. (You will have to work this out from the statement of financial position figures and depreciation and any other information you are given on additions and disposals)
9) Work out cash inflow outflow from financing
   Increase in share capital/loans = inflow (add).
   Equity dividends ***paid***
10) The total of all of these items should equal the change in the cash balance from last year.

Understanding the Statement of cash flows

The operating activities section of the statement of cash flows shows the amount of cash that has been generated from operating activities. These are activities like receiving payments from customers, making payments to suppliers and paying all the normal expenses of the business. The operating cash flow is calculated by starting with the profit before interest and tax (PBIT) figure from the income statement. This shows the amount of profit that has been generated from operations. This figure must be adjusted for any amounts that have been included in profit but have not turned into cash.

The first item that has been included in profit but is not a cash flow is depreciation. When a non-current asset is acquired the purchase price is paid to the seller. This transaction does involve cash being paid out and will feature in the investing activities section of the statement of cash flows. The non-current asset is then depreciated over its useful life. This involves reducing the value of the non-current asset in the statement of financial position and charging depreciation in the income statement (see Chapter 7.) This entry does not involve any transfer of cash. Depreciation is a 'non-cash' expense and must be added back to profit figure in order to calculate the businesses' operating cash flow.

Profit figures also include sales that have not yet been received in cash and purchases and expenses that have not yet been paid for. Adjustments are made for these items by examining the changes in receivables and payables from the start to the end of the accounting period. For example, suppose the sales figure for a firm was €100,000 and that receivables were €20,000 at the start of the year and €30,000 at the end of the year. In this case, the firm would have received €90,000 in cash during the year. Because receivables have increased by €10,000 during the year we have €10,000 of 'extra' receivables that were not paid during the year. Here receivables have increased and this means less cash was received than sales recorded in the income statement. This gives the general rule that an increase in receivables is a use of cash or a negative item in the statement of cash flows. Similar logic can be used for payables. Using this shortcut we can adjust for any changes in the amount of credit that the business is giving and receiving. A positive change in receivables is a use of cash and a positive change in payables is a source of cash.

The amount of cash paid out of the business for interest and taxation is also shown in the statement of cash flows. Being that the statement of cash flows starts with profit before interest and tax these items have no been included in these figures. The amount of cash paid out for these amounts must be calculated and included as a cash outflow in the operating cash flow section of the statement. The income statement shows how much interest and taxation have been incurred during the accounting period. This is not necessarily the amount that has been paid out in cash. In order to estimate the amount paid out in cash the statement of financial position must be examined to see if any interest or taxation were due at the start and end of the accounting period. For example, if the statement of financial position shows that €10,000 of taxation was due at the start of the accounting period and €15,000 was due at the end of the accounting period and the income statement shows that a tax charge of €60,000 was incurred during the year then the amount of taxation paid during the accounting period can be worked out. Take the €10,000 owed at the start of the period and add on the €60,000 tax charge for the period. This gives a total of €70,000 which would be owed at the end of the accounting period if we had not made any payments. However, the statement of financial position shows that only €15,000 is owed at the end of the accounting period so we must have paid €55,000 during the accounting period. This is the amount that goes into the statement of cash flows as a taxation outflow.

The investment section of the statement of cash flows shows the cash outflows from acquiring non-current assets and the inflows from disposing of non-current assets. The figures for this section must be worked out from the changes in the non-current assets section of the statement of financial position and the depreciation figure and any profit and losses on disposals of assets in the income statement. For example, if the net book value (see Chapter 7) of the total non-current assets is €100,000 at the start of the accounting period and €120,000 at the end of the accounting period and the charge for the depreciation in the income statement is €10,000 then assuming no disposals €30,000 worth of non-current assets must have been acquired. This figure would appear as an outflow in the investment section of the statement of cash flows.

The financing section of the statement of cash flows shows the cash inflows and outflows from issuing equity (see Chapter 8) and issuing and repaying debt (see Chapter 9). These inflows and outflows are calculated by examining the changes in equity share capital and debt in the statement of financial position between the start and end of the accounting period. Note that the change in retained income is not taken into this section as the change in retained income is equal to the profit from the financial year from the income statement. This profit has already been dealt with in the operating cash flow section of the statement.

When all of the sections of the statement of cash flows have been prepared all of the cash inflows and outflows are totalled. This amount is called the increase or decrease in cash. This should be equal to the change in the cash balances on the statement of financial position. In this way the statement of cash flows explains the change in the business's cash. It shows how much of the change in cash is explained by operations, by investing and by financing.

Preparation of a Statement of cash flows

The statements of financial position of **Rochester plc** for the years ended 31 December 2006 and 2005 are given below, together with the summarised income statement for 2006.

Table 13.6 Information for Rochester plc

Statement of financial position of Rochester plc as at 31 December

ASSETS	**2006**	**2005**
Non-current assets	**€'000**	**€'000**
Land	250	100
Buildings	500	50
Plant and Machinery	765	707
Total non-current assets	1,515	857
Current assets		
Inventory	320	278
Receivables	234	290
Cash	20	140
Total current assets	574	708
Total assets	2,089	1,565
EQUITY		
Ordinary Share Capital (€1 shares)	220	100
Retained income	1,386	1,149
Total equity	1,606	1,249
LIABILITIES		
Non-current liabilities		
Long term loans	200	-
Current liabilities		
Trade payables	213	201
Taxation	60	114
Interest	10	1
Total current liabilities	283	316
Total equity and liabilities	2,089	1,565

Table 13.6 (cont.)
Income Statement of Rochester plc for year ended 31/12/06 (Extract)

	€'000
Profit before finance costs	385
Interest	(18)
Profit before taxation	367
Taxation	(75)
Profit for the financial year	292

The following information is also provided:

1. Profit for the year is after charging:

	€
Depreciation on buildings	10,000
Depreciation on plant & machinery	102,000

2. There were no disposals of land or buildings during the year.
3. Plant which cost €50,000 and had a net book value of €30,000 was disposed of during the year. A profit of €2,000 was made on this disposal.
4. Dividends of €55,000 were paid during the year.

The statement of cash flows for Rochester plc for the year ended 31 December 2006 is given in Table 13.7.

Table 13.7
Rochester plc Statement of cash flows
for the year ended 31 December 2006

	Solution Note	€'000
Operations		
Operating profit (Profit before Interest and Tax)	1	385
Depreciation charges	2	112
Profit on disposal	3	(2)
Increase in inventory	4	(42)
Decrease in receivables	4	56
Increase in payables	4	12
Interest paid (1+18-10)	5	(9)
Tax paid (114+75-60)	6	(129)
Operating cash flow	7	383
Investment		
Payments to acquire non-current assets W1 (150+460+190)	8	(800)
Receipts from sales of non-current assets	8	32
Financing		
Equity dividends paid	9	(55)
Issue of ordinary share capital	10	120
Issue of long term loan	10	200
Decrease in cash		(120)

We will now analyse how each of the numbers in the statement of cash flows was derived from the financial statements.

1. *Take Profit before Interest and Tax*
   This is usually given in the income statement although in some questions you have to work it out from the change in retained earnings in the statement of financial position. In this question, it is straightforward and is the first figure in the income statement (€385,000)

2. *Add back depreciation, loss on sale of assets*
   Depreciation must be added back because it is a ***non-cash*** expense. The bank account decreases when the asset is purchased but annual depreciation has no effect on the bank account. Therefore in cash flow terms we show the purchase of a non-current asset in the statement of cash flows in the year of purchase but we exclude depreciation.

Note 2 states that depreciation on buildings is €10,000 and depreciation on plant and machinery is €102,000.

3. *Subtract profit on sale of asset*
Note 2 states that the profit on sale of asset is €2,000. The profit on sale of a non-current asset has no effect on the bank account. What does have an effect is the money received for the non-current asset. The proceeds are taken into account in the capital expenditure section (see note 8 below).

4. *Show inflows and outflows from current assets and liabilities*
Increase in receivables/inventory = outflow (subtract)
Increase in payables = inflow (add)

5. *Work out interest* **paid.** *(You may have to work this out using interest due on the statements of financial position and interest charged in the P&L)*
We need to identify three figures (1) interest due at the start of the year; (2) interest 'clocked up' during the year; and (3) interest due at the end of the year. The interest 'clocked up' during the year can be found in the income statement (€18,000). You can see from the current liabilities section of the statement of financial position that interest of €1,000 was due at the start of the year and tax of €10,000 was due at the end. If we owed €1,000 at the start and 'clocked up' extra interest of €18,000 during the year we would have owed €19,000 at the end if we did not pay any interest. But the statement of financial position says we only owe €10,000 at the end of the year. This must mean we paid interest of €9,000 during the year.

6. *Work out tax* **paid.** *(You may have to work this out using tax due on the statements of financial position and tax charged in the P&L)*
We need to identify three figures (1) tax due at the start of the year; (2) tax 'clocked up' during the year; and (3) tax due at the end of the year. The tax 'clocked up' during the year can be found in the income statement (€75,000). You can see from the current liabilities section of the statement of financial position that tax of €114,000 was due at the start of the year and tax of €60,000 was due at the end. If we owed €114,000 at the start and 'clocked up' extra tax of €75,000 during the year we would have owed €189,000 at the end if we did not pay any tax. But the statement of financial position says we only owe €60,000 at the end of the year. This must mean we paid tax of €129,000 during the year.

⇨ Cash outflow of €110,000 for tax paid.

7. This gives cash inflow/outflow from operations.

8. *Work out additions/disposals of non-current assets. (You will have to work this out from the statement of financial position figures and depreciation and any information you are given on additions and disposals)*

   We have to work out why the non-current asset values changed from 2005 to 2006.

   Look at land first. The net book value (cost less accumulated depreciation) of land went from €100,000 to €250,000). This could be explained by three things (1) additions to our holdings of land (2) disposals of our holding of land (3) depreciation on land. However, we know land is not depreciated so this rules out number (3). We are told (note 2 to question) that we did not dispose of any land so that rules out number (2). This implies that the whole change (€150,000) must be additions to our holding of land.

   ⇨ We purchased land of €150,000 => a cash outflow in the capital expenditure section.

   Look at Buildings now. The net book value (cost less accumulated depreciation) of buildings went from €50,000 to €500,000). This could be explained by three things (1) additions to our holdings of buildings (2) disposals of our holding of buildings (3) depreciation on buildings. We are told (note 2 to question) that we did not dispose of any buildings so that rules out number (2). We are told (note 1 to question) that buildings have been depreciated by €10,000. This means we must have purchased buildings for €460,000 and then charged depreciation of €10,000. This explains the change in NBV from €50,000 to €450,000.

   ⇨ We purchased buildings of €460,000 => a cash outflow in the capital expenditure section.

   Finally consider plant and machinery. The net book value (cost less accumulated depreciation) of P&M went from €707,000 to €765,000). This could be explained by three things (1) additions to our holdings of P&M (2) disposals of our holding of P&M (3) depreciation on P&M. We are told (note 3 to question) that we disposed of plant with a net book value of €30,000. Remember that in this question all of the non-current asset figures are stated in terms of net book values. In some question you have to split out the cost from the accumulated depreciation. This means that the net book value of P&M went down by €30,000 due to the disposal. We are told (note 1 to question) that P&M has been depreciated by €102,000. This means we must have purchased P&M for €190,000. The change in NBV from €707,000 to €765,000 is explained by (1) purchasing P&M €190,000; (2) Selling plant with a NBV of €30,000; (3) depreciation of €102,000.

⇨ We purchased P&M for €190,000 => a cash outflow in the capital expenditure section.

Next we have to work out how much we got for the asset we sold. We know that the asset had a net book value of €30,000 and that we made a profit of €2,000 on the disposal. This means we must have received €32,000 for the asset.

⇨ We sold P&M for €32,000 => a cash inflow in the capital expenditure section.

9. We are told that Rochester paid dividends of €55,000 during the year.

10. Work out cash inflow outflow from financing
Increase in share capital/loans = inflow (add).

Interpreting a Statement of cash flows

The statement of cash flows provides information about the cash flows into and out of the business that is not provided elsewhere in the financial statements. The statement shows where the business got cash during the year and where it was spent.

The operations section of the statement of cash flows shows how much cash has been generated from the day-to-day operations of the business. The business receives cash when customers pay for goods. Cash has to be paid to suppliers and to the government and banks.

Summary

The statement of cash flows shows the movements in the cash balance during the year.

Chapter 13 Exercises

Exercise 13.1

The statements of financial position of **Grove plc** for the years ended 31 December 2005 and 2004 are given below, together with the summarised profit and loss account for 2005.

Statement of financial position of Grove plc as at 31 December

	2005 €'000	2005 €'000	2004 €'000	2004 €'000
Non-current assets				
Land		500		500
Buildings		1,780		400
Plant and Machinery		980		160
		3,260		1,060
Current assets				
Inventory	450		190	
Receivables	340		250	
Bank	120		1,100	
	910		1,540	
Total assets		4,170		2,600
Equity				
Equity Share Capital (€1 shares)		1,500		1,000
Share premium		1,000		750
Retained income		895		431
		3,395		2,181
Non-current liabilities				
Long term debt		500		180
Current liabilities				
Trade payables	200		180	
Taxation	35		29	
Accruals	40	275	30	239
Total liabilities and equity		4,170		2,600

Income statement of Grove plc for year ended 31/12/2005 (Extract)

	€'000
Profit before finance costs	619
Interest	(30)
	589
Taxation	(65)
Profit for the financial year	524

The following information is also provided:

1. Profit for the year is after charging -

	€
Depreciation - Buildings	10,000
- Plant & Machinery	40,000
Loss on sale of plant	20,000

2. There were no disposals of land or buildings during the year.

3. Plant which cost €210,000 and had a net book value of €40,000 was disposed of during the year.

4. Dividends of €60,000 were paid during the year.

REQUIRED:

(i) Prepare a statement of cash flows, in accordance with IAS 7, for Grove plc for the year ended 31 December 2005.

(ii) In the Annual Report of Grove plc the Chief Executive Officer of the company stated

"Our mission at Grove plc is to become a leading manufacturer of consumer products. In order to achieve this mission we have substantially upgraded our manufacturing facilities and systems. This substantial investment in our future will ensure that we can continue to produce high quality products for our customers."

Discuss whether this statement is in accordance with the statement of cash flows for Grove plc. Analyse how Grove plc financed the investments mentioned in the above quotation.

Solutions to Exercises

Chapter 1 Solutions

Exercise 1.1

Classify each of the following items as an asset, a liability or equity:

Item	**Classification**
Buildings	***Non-current asset***
A bank loan	***Current liability***
Cash in the bank	***Current asset***
Payables	***Current liability***
Tax due to the government	***Current liability***
Receivables	***Current asset***
Inventory	***Current asset***
Share capital	***Equity***
Retained income	***Equity***

Exercise 1.3

Which of the following items would meet the definition of an asset of ABC plc? Provide an explanation of your answer in each case.

- Land owned by ABC plc.

Land is an asset. It provides economic benefits of occupation (or sale proceeds) in the future. It is controlled by the enterprise through their ownership.

- A car owned by Jane Murphy who is a director of ABC plc.

This car is not an asset of ABC plc. It is not controlled by ABC and does not provide economic benefits.

- Rent owed to ABC plc by DEF plc.

As long as this debt is enforceable then it is an asset of ABC plc because future economic benefits should flow from it.

- €1,000 which will be owed to ABC plc by TRF plc when ABC plc delivers goods to TRF plc.

This is not an asset. There is no past event that gives rise to an enforceable debt and future economic benefits.

- €10,000 which has been spent on researching a new product that ABC plc will manufacture.

This is a grey area. If the future economic benefits from the research are certain enough then it may be an asset.

- €50,000 which has been spent on repairing the roof of ABC plc's warehouse.

This is a grey area. If the repairs are just putting the resource controlled by the enterprise back to their previous state then this expenditure is not an asset. If new future benefits are created (i.e. the roof is improved) then it may be an asset.

Exercise 1.4

For each of the following 6 companies, one figure is missing. The missing figure can be calculated using the accounting equation of:

Assets = Liabilities + Equity

	Assets	**Liabilities**	**Equity**
1.	295	117	***178***
2.	11,961	***8,746***	3,215
3.	**4,727**	1,911	2,816
4.	106,412	62,372	***44,040***
5.	?	9,383	?
6.	19,495	12,713	**6,782**

No 5. can't be solved.

Exercise 1.5

Statement of financial position

	A plc	B plc	C plc
Non-current assets:	€	€	€
Land and buildings	2,500	6,000	2,000
Plant and machinery	2,000	1,000	6,000
Total non-current assets	4,500	7,000	8,000
Current assets:			
Inventory/Stock	400	2,000	3,500
Receivables (Debtors)	1,300	3,000	1,500
Loan receivable	900	0	2,000
Cash/Bank	100	200	0
Total current assets	2,700	5,200	7,000
Total assets	7,200	12,200	15,000
Equity			
Share capital of €1 each	3,000	5,000	? 7,500
Retained	1,200	? 5,200	4,000
Total equity	4,200	10,200	11,500
Non-current liabilities			
Long term loans	2,000	1,000	0
Current liabilities:			
Payables (Creditors)	300	1,000	2,000
Bank overdraft	700	0	1,500
Total liabilities	3,000	2,000	3,500
Total equity and liabilities	7,200	12,200	15,000

Exercise 1.6

Statement of financial position of Cosmos Ltd. as at	**31/3/X1**
Non-current assets:	**€**
Land	105,000
Buildings	110,000
Plant and machinery	185,000
Total non-current assets	400,000
Current assets:	
Inventory	40,000
Receivables	90,000
Cash/Bank	? 45,000
Total current assets	175,000
Total assets	575,000
Equity	
Share capital of €1 each	250,000
Retained	65,000
Total equity	315,000
Non-current liabilities	
Long term loans	? 200,000
Current liabilities:	
Payables (Creditors)	60,000
Total liabilities	260,000
Total equity and liabilities	575,000

Chapter 2

Exercise 2.1 Solution

Murphy Machine Tools Ltd.

			20x6
Liquidity			
Current ratio			
Current Assets		1,707	
Current Liabilities		679	
			2.5 :1
Acid-test ratio			
Current Assets - Inventory	1,707 -	450	
Current Liabilities		679	**1.9 :1**
Gearing			
Debt/equity percentage			
Non-current borrowings		651	
Total equity		4,109	**15.8%**
Profitability			
Return on capital employed			
Profit before finance costs		995	
Capital employed	4,109 +	651	**20.9%**
Return on equity			
Profit before tax		943	
Total equity		4,109	**22.9%**

Operating ratios

Gross profit percentage

Gross profit		1,417		
Revenue		4,523	**31.3%**	

Net profit percentage

Profit before finance costs		995		
Revenue		4,523	**22.0%**	

Inventory days

Average inventory*		450		
Cost of sales		3,106	**14.5%**	
x days (365)			**52.9**	**Days**

* use closing inventory as opening n/a.

Receivables days

Receivables x 365	1,012 x	365		
Revenue*		4,523	**81.7**	**Days**

* Use revenue as credit sales n/a

Payables days

Payables x 365	342 x	365		
Cost of sales		3,106	**40.2**	**Days**

Discussion

Profitability

The company manufactures machine tools which is probably a reasonably high gross margin industry. It should be generating a healthy gross profit margin but may be capital intensive. The gross margin of 31% seems reasonable for this industry. A return on shareholders funds of 20% is also reasonable. There is little difference between the return on equity and the return on capital employed which is probably because of the low gearing.

Liquidity

Liquidity is the ability of the firm to meet its debts as they fall due. The current ratio of 2.51 and acid test ratio of 1.85 are very strong. This seems to be caused by the high level of receivables. As the debtors days of 81 days is quite high the firm may want to investigate why the receivables are not paying their debts on time. The firm seems to have a high cash position of €245,000 which should mean they are bale to pay short term obligations. The stock holding period of 52 days seems reasonable for a firm in this industry.

Gearing

The firm has long term loans of €651,000 in comparison to equity capital of €4,109,000. It would seem that the firm is lowly geared. However more data is required to be sure that the firm could support a higher level of debt. For example if the firm is in a cyclical industry it may not be prudent to take on more debt.

Exercise 2.2 Solution

Irish Metal Cases Limited

Liquidity

				20x6	
Current ratio	Current Assets		5,276		
	Current Liabilities		5,180		
				1.0	**:1**
Acid-test ratio					
	Current Assets - Inventory	5,276 -	2,045		
	Current Liabilities		5,180	**0.6**	**:1**

Gearing

Debt/equity percentage

Non-current borrowings		8,309	
Total equity		21,708	**38.3%**

Profitability

Return on capital employed

Profit before finance costs		1,631	
Capital employed	21,708 +	8,309	**5.4%**

Return on equity

Profit before tax	791	
Total equity	21,708	**3.6%**

Operating ratios

		20x6		20x5
Gross profit percentage				
Gross profit	8,053		5,864	
Revenue	20,132	**40.0%**	16,754	**35.0%**

Net profit percentage

Profit before finance costs	1,631		1,526	
Revenue	20,132	**8.1%**	16,754	**9.1%**

Inventory days	Average inventory*	2,045	
	Cost of sales	12,079	**16.9%**
	x days (365)		**61.8**
	* use closing inventory as opening n/a.		**Days**

Receivables days	Receivables x 365	3,219 x	365		
	Revenue*		20,132	**58.4**	**Days**
	* Use revenue as credit sales n/a				
Payables days					
	Payables x 365	4,567 x	365		
	Cost of sales		12,079	**138.0**	**Days**

Students should prepare a discussion of these ratios.

No solution is provided for Exercise 2.3

Exercise 2.4
Saw-it and Hammer-down Solution

(a)

Saw-it has a higher gross profit percentage (31.55%) than Hammer-down. This could be caused by better purchasing, higher sales prices, better product mix or lower inventory losses. Saw-it does have higher sales than Hammer-down so maybe it has better locations or more shop space. However, Saw-it's operating costs are higher leaving both firms with equal operating profit as a percentage of sales. Hammer-down has made a profit on the sale of an asset. Saw-it has much higher finance costs (interest) due to its much higher level of debt. Saw-it's profit for the financial year is a lower % of sales mainly due to its higher finance costs.

(b)

Saw-it

Return on equity	= Profit Before Tax ÷ Total Equity % = 3,617 / 5,000	72.3%
Return on capital employed	= Profit Before Finance Costs ÷ Capital Employed % = 4,817 / 25,000	19.3%

Hammer-down

Return on equity	= Profit Before Tax ÷ Total Equity % = 3,880 / 18,000	21.6%
Return on capital employed	= Profit Before Finance Costs ÷ Capital Employed % = 4,000 / 20,000	20.0%

Saw-it has a much larger return on equity than return on capital employed. This is because Saw-it is mainly financed using debt rather than equity. It is trading on a small amount of equity which boosts the returns to the equity holders. The return on equity and return on capital employed is similar for Hammer-down because it only has a small amount of debt.

Both Hammer-down and Saw-it seem to be making good returns from their businesses. Returns of 20% on capital employed compare favourably with returns on a deposit account of 3%-5% and returns on other potential investments.

(c)

Liquidity is the ability of a business to pay its debts as they fall due. It is a short term concept and is concerned with the short terms resources and obligations of the business. These items can be found in the current assets and current liabilities sections of the statement of financial position. A high bank balance means that the business is unlikely to have liquidity problems. Inventory, receivables and payables turnover should be used to access the firms cash cycle. The current ratio and acid-test ratio can be used to access the margin of safety of current assets over current liabilities.

Chapter 3

Exercise 3.1 Solution

Fill in the missing entries in the following table:

	Debit	**Credit**
Increase in	Asset	Liability
Decrease in	Liability	Asset

Exercise 3.2

Ms. Beancounter started a new business by forming a limited company Beancounter Ltd. Her first 3 transactions are given below.

Transaction Number	**Date**	**Description**
1	1 Jan	Beancounter Ltd. is formed as a limited company and Ms. Beancounter invests €1,000 for 1,000 shares of €1 each
2	1 Jan	Beancounter Ltd. receives a loan of €500 from the Bank of Dublin. This amount is received immediately into Beancounter Ltd.'s bank account.
3	2 Jan	Beancounter Ltd. buys a second hand van for €1,000 and pays by cheque.

(a) Prepare the statement of financial position of Beancounter Ltd. as at the 2nd of January. Use the following table to trace through the transactions.

	Tx. 1	**Tx. 2**	**Tx. 3**	**Statement of financial position as at 2nd January**
Assets				
Van			1,000 dr.	1,000 dr.
Bank	1,000 dr.	500 dr.	1,000 cr.	500 dr.
=				1,500 dr.
Equity				
Issued share capital Shares of €1.00 each	1,000 cr.			1,000 cr.
+ Liabilities				
Bank loan		500 cr.		500 cr.
				1,500 cr.

(b) Prepare journal entries for each of the transactions

Tx. 1

Date	Account	Debit	Credit
1/1	Bank	1,000	
1/1	Equity share capital		1,000

Being issue of 1,000 shares at €1 each

Tx. 2

Date	Account	Debit	Credit
1/1	Bank	500	
1/1	Bank loan		500

Being receipt of loan

Tx. 3

Date	Account	Debit	Credit
2/1	Van	1,000	
2/1	Bank		1,000

Being purchase of van

(c) Post each of the journal entries to T accounts using the template below. Balance each T account.

Bank

Debit			**Credit**		
Date	*Account*	*Amount*	*Date*	*Account*	*Amount*
1/1	Issued share capital	1,000	2/1	Van	1,000
1/1	Bank loan	500	2/1	Balance	500
		1,500			1,500
2/1	Balance	500			

Van

Debit			**Credit**		
Date	*Account*	*Amount*	*Date*	*Account*	*Amount*
2/1	*Bank*	*1,000*	2/1	Balance	1,000
		1,000			1,000
2/1	Balance	1,000			

Bank Loan

Debit			**Credit**		
Date	*Account*	*Amount*	*Date*	*Account*	*Amount*
2/1	Balance	500	1/1	Bank	500
		500			500
			2/1	Balance	500

Issued Share Capital

Debit			**Credit**		
Date	*Account*	*Amount*	*Date*	*Account*	*Amount*
1/1	Balance	1,000	1/1	Bank	1,000
		1,000			1,000
			1/1	Balance	1,000

(d) Extract a trial balance from the T accounts

Trial Balance

Account	**Debit**	**Credit**
Bank	500	
Van	1,000	
Bank loan		500
Issued share capital		1,000
	1,500	1,500

Chapter 4

Exercise 4.1 Solution

Beancounter Ltd. started to trade in January. The transactions are given below:

Transaction Number	Date	Description
4	3 Jan	Beancounter Ltd. buys in widgets for €500 in cash.
5	4 Jan	Beancounter Ltd. sells all of the widgets for €1,000 in cash.
6	5 Jan	Beancounter Ltd. pays wages to Ms. Beancounter of €200 in cash.

(a) Prepare the statement of financial position of Beancounter Ltd. as at the 5th of January. Use the following table to trace through the transactions.

Statement of financial position as at 5 January

	As at 2/1	Tx. 4	Tx. 5	Tx. 6		
Assets						
Van	1,000 dr.				1,000 dr.	
Bank	500 dr.	500 cr.	1,000 dr.	200 cr.	800 dr.	
=					1,800 dr.	
Equity						
Issued share capital Shares of €1.00 each	1,000 cr.				1,000 cr.	
Retained income					300 cr.	***← from***
+ Liabilities						***Income***
Bank loan	500 cr.				500 cr.	***State-ment***

Income Statement for the period 1 January – 5 January

Revenue		1,000 cr.		1,000 cr.	***To***
Purchases	500 dr.			500 dr.	***Ret-ained***
Wages			200 dr	200 dr.	***income***
Profit				300 cr.	**←**

(b) Prepare journal entries for each of the transactions

Tx. 4

Date	Account	Debit	Credit
3/1	Purchases	500	
3/1	Bank		500

Being ***purchase of widgets***

Tx. 5

Date	Account	Debit	Credit
4/1	Bank	1,000	
4/1	Sales		1,000

Being ***sale of widgets***

Tx. 6

Date	Account	Debit	Credit
5/1	Wages	200	
5/1	Bank		200

Being ***wages***

(c) Post each of the journal entries to T accounts using the template below. Balance each T account.

Debit — **Bank** — **Credit**

Date	*Account*	*Amount*	*Date*	*Account*	*Amount*
1/1	Issued share capital	1,000	2/1	Van	1,000
1/1	Bank loan	500	3/1	Purchases	500
4/1	Sales	1,000	5/1	Wages	200
			5/1	Balance	800
		2,500			2,500
5/1	Balance	800			

Debit — **Van** — **Credit**

Date	*Account*	*Amount*	*Date*	*Account*	*Amount*
2/1	Bank	1,000	5/1	Balance	1,000
		1,000			1,000
5/1	Balance	1,000			

Debit — **Bank Loan** — **Credit**

Date	*Account*	*Amount*	*Date*	*Account*	*Amount*
5/1	Balance	500	1/1	Bank	500
		500			500
			5/1	Balance	500

Debit — **Issued Share Capital** — **Credit**

Date	*Account*	*Amount*	*Date*	*Account*	*Amount*
5/1	Balance	1,000	1/1	Bank	1,000
		1,000			1,000
			5/1	Balance	1,000

Debit		**Purchases**			**Credit**
Date	*Account*	*Amount*	*Date*	*Account*	*Amount*
3/1	Bank	500	5/1	Balance	500
		500			500
5/1	Balance	500			

Debit		**Sales**			**Credit**
Date	*Account*	*Amount*	*Date*	*Account*	*Amount*
5/1	Balance	1,000	4/1	Bank	1,000
		1,000			1,000
			5/1	Balance	1,000

Debit		**Wages**			**Credit**
Date	*Account*	*Amount*	*Date*	*Account*	*Amount*
5/1	Bank	200	5/1	Balance	200
		200			200
5/1	Balance	200			

(d) Extract a trial balance from the T accounts

Trial Balance

Account	**Debit**	**Credit**
Bank	800	
Van	1,000	
Purchases	500	
Sales		1,000
Wages	200	
Bank loan		500
Issued share capital		1,000
	2,500	2,500

Chapter 5

Exercise 5.1 Solution

(a) Prepare the income statement and statement of financial position of Columbus Ltd. using the list of transactions above.

Columbus Ltd. Income Statement for the period ended:

	31 January
Revenue	*25,000*
Less expenses	
Materials cost	*(10,000)*
Motor vehicle hire	*(700)*
Rent expense	*(2,500)*
Interest expense	*(120)*
Profit for the financial period	*11,680*

Note (...) signify negative amounts

Columbus Ltd. - Calculation of the Bank balance at the end of January

Date	Description	Amount €
1. Jan	Opening bank account	
	Bank balance	0
1/1	Issued share capital rec'd	30,000
1/1	Bank loan rec'd	20,000
2/1	Motor car rental	(700)
2/1	Premises rental	(2,500)
3/1	Materials cost	(10,000)
3/1-30/1	Sales	25,000
30 Jan	Interest expense	(120)
31 Jan	Bank balance	61,680

Columbus Ltd. Statement of financial position as at:

	31 January
Assets	
Bank	61,680
Liabilities	
Bank loan	(20,000)
	41,680
Equity	
Issued share capital	30,000
Retained income	11,680
	41,680

(b) Prepare journal entries for each of the transactions

Tx. 1

Date	Account	Debit	Credit
1/1	Bank	30,000	
1/1	Issued share capital		30,000

Being issue of share capital

Tx. 2

Date	Account	Debit	Credit
1/1	Bank	20,000	
1/1	Bank loan		20,000

Being receipt of bank loan

Tx. 3

Date	Account	Debit	Credit
2/1	Motor vehicle rent (IS)	700	
2/1	Bank		700

Being rent of motor vehicle

Tx. 4

Date	Account	Debit	Credit
2/1	Premises rent	2,500	
2/1	Bank		2,500

Being premises rent for one month (January)

Tx. 5

Date	Account	Debit	Credit
3/1	Materials cost	10,000	
3/1	Bank		10,000

Being purchase of materials

Tx. 6

Date	**Account**	**Debit**	**Credit**
3/1-30/1	Bank	25,000	
3/1-30/1	Sales		25,000

Being sales for January

Tx. 7

Date	**Account**	**Debit**	**Credit**
30/1	Interest expense	120	
30/1	Bank		120

Being interest expense

(c) Record each of the transactions in T accounts

Debit		**Bank (BS)**			**Credit**
Date	*Account*	*Amount*	*Date*	*Account*	*Amount*
1/1	Issued share capital	30,000	2/1	Motor rental	700
1/1	Bank loan	20,000	2/1	Premises rental	2,500
30/1	Sales	25,000	3/1	Materials cost	10,000
			30/1	Interest	120
			31/1	Balance	61,680
		75,000			75,000
31/1	Balance	61,680			

Debit		**Materials Costs (IS)**			**Credit**
Date	*Account*	*Amount*	*Date*	*Account*	*Amount*
3/1	Bank	10,000	31/1	Balance	10,000
		10,000			10,000
31/1	Balance	10,000			

Debit		**Revenue/Sales (IS)**			**Credit**
Date	*Account*	*Amount*	*Date*	*Account*	*Amount*
31/1	Balance	25,000	30/1	Bank	25,000
		25,000			25,000
			31/1	Balance	25,000

Debit		**Motor Van Rental (IS)**			**Credit**
Date	*Account*	*Amount*	*Date*	*Account*	*Amount*
2/1	Bank	700	31/1	Balance	700
		700			700
31/1	Balance	700			

Debit — **Premises Rental (IS)** — **Credit**

Date	*Account*	*Amount*	*Date*	*Account*	*Amount*
2/1	Bank	2,500	31/1	Balance	2,500
		2,500			2,500
31/1	Balance	2,500			

Debit — **Interest Expense (IS)** — **Credit**

Date	*Account*	*Amount*	*Date*	*Account*	*Amount*
2/1	Bank	120	31/1	Balance	120
		120			120
31/1	Balance	120			

Debit — **Bank Loan (BS)** — **Credit**

Date	*Account*	*Amount*	*Date*	*Account*	*Amount*
31/1	Balance	20,000	1/1	Bank	20,000
		20,000			20,000
			31/1	Balance	20,000

Debit — **Issued Share Capital (BS)** — **Credit**

Date	*Account*	*Amount*	*Date*	*Account*	*Amount*
31/1	Balance	30,000	1/1	Bank	30,000
		30,000			30,000
			31/1	Balance	30,000

(d) Prepare a trial balance

Trial Balance for Columbus Ltd. as at 31st January

Account	***Debit***	***Credit***
Bank	61,680	
Materials cost	10,000	
Revenue		25,000
Motor vehicle rental	700	
Premises rental	2,500	
Interest expense	120	
Bank loan		20,000
Issued share capital		30,000
	75,000	75,000

Chapter 6
Exercise 6.2 Solution

Danish Pastry Ltd.
Statement of financial position as at 31 December

	20x6	Tx. 1	Tx. 2	Tx. 3	Tx. 4	Tx.5	Tx. 6	T/F Profit to Ret. Inc.	Revised at 31/12/x6
	€	€	€	€	€	€	€		€
Non-Current Assets									
Property, plant and equipment	11,000								11,000
Current Assets									
Inventory	4,000								4,000
Receivables	4,000		1,000 dr						5,000
Prepayments							250 dr		250
Bank	5,500			300 dr					5,800
	24,500								26,050
Equity									
Equity share capital	10,000								10,000
Retained Income (op. 9,700+2,300)	12,000							**350 cr**	12,350
	22,000								22,350
Current liabilities									
Payables	2,500	700 cr							3,200
Accruals					300 cr	200cr			500
	24,500								26,050

Danish Pastry Ltd.
Income Statement for the year ended 31 December

	20x6	**Tx. 1**	**Tx. 2**	**Tx. 3**	**Tx. 4**	**Tx.5**	**Tx. 6**	**T/F Profit to Ret. Inc.**	**Revised at 31/12/x6**
	€	€	€	€	€	€	€		€
Revenue	100,000		1,000 cr	300 cr					101,300
Less cost of sales	(75,000)	700dr							(75,700)
Gross profit	25,000								25,600
Wages	(3,000)				300 dr				(3,300)
Light & heat	(1,200)					200 dr			(1,400)
Insurance	(500)						250 cr		(250)
All other expenses	(18,000)								(18,000)
		700 dr	1,000 cr	300cr	300 dr	200 dr	250 cr	**350 cr**	
Net profit	2,300								2,650

Journal Entries

Tx. 1

Date	Account	Debit	Credit
…	Purchases	700	
…	Payables		700

Being purchase of goods for resale

Tx. 2

Date	Account	Debit	Credit
…	Receivables	1,000	
…	Revenue		1,000

Being credit sale

Tx. 3

Date	Account	Debit	Credit
…	Bank	300	
…	Revenue		300

Being cash sale

Tx. 4

Date	Account	Debit	Credit
…	Wage expense (IS)	300	
…	Accruals (BS)		300

Being wages due at y/e

Tx. 5

Date	Account	Debit	Credit
…	Light and heat expense (IS)	200	
…	Accruals (BS)		200

Being ESB due at y/e

Tx. 6

Date	Account	Debit	Credit
…	Prepayments	250	
…	Insurance expense		250

Being insurance prepaid at y/e

Exhibit 3 Danish Pastry Ltd.'s T Accounts

Debit **Receivables (BS)** **Credit**

Date	*Account*	*Amount*	*Date*	*Account*	*Amount*
...	Bal	**4,000**			
...	Revenue	1,000			
			...	Bal	5,000
		5,000			5,000
...	Bal	5,000			

Debit **Prepayments (BS)** **Credit**

Date	*Account*	*Amount*	*Date*	*Account*	*Amount*
...	Insurance	250	...	Bal	250
		250			250
...	Bal	250			

Debit **Bank (BS)** **Credit**

Date	*Account*	*Amount*	*Date*	*Account*	*Amount*
...	Bal	**5,500**			
...	Revenue	300			
			...	Bal	
		5,800			5,800
...	Bal	5,800			

Debit **Payables (BS)** **Credit**

Date	*Account*	*Amount*	*Date*	*Account*	*Amount*
			...	Bal	**2,500**
...	Bal	3,200	...	Purchases	700
		3,200			3,200
			...	Bal	3,200

Debit **Accruals (BS)** **Credit**

Date	*Account*	*Amount*	*Date*	*Account*	*Amount*
			…	Wage expense	300
…	Bal	500	…	Light & heat	200
		500			500
			…	Bal	500

Debit **Revenue (IS)** **Credit**

Date	*Account*	*Amount*	*Date*	*Account*	*Amount*
			…	Bal	**100,000**
			…	Receivables	1,000
…	Bal	101,300	…	Bank	300
		101,300			101,300
			…	Bal	101,300

Debit **Purchases (IS)** **Credit**

Date	*Account*	*Amount*	*Date*	*Account*	*Amount*
…	Bal	**75,000**			
…	Payables	700	…	Bal	75,700
		75,700			
…	Bal	75,700			

Debit **Wages (IS)** **Credit**

Date	*Account*	*Amount*	*Date*	*Account*	*Amount*
…	Bal	**3,000**			
…	Accruals	300	…	Bal	3,300
		3,300			3,300
…	Bal	3,300			

Debit **Light & Heat (IS)** **Credit**

Date	*Account*	*Amount*	*Date*	*Account*	*Amount*
…	Bal	**1,200**			
…	Accruals	200	…	Bal	1,400
		1,400			1,400
…	Bal	1,400			

Debit		**Insurance (IS)**			**Credit**
Date	*Account*	*Amount*	*Date*	*Account*	*Amount*
...	Bal	**500**	...	Prepayment	250
			...	Bal	250
		500			500
...	Bal	250			

NOTES:

This is an incomplete set of T Accounts. You are only provided with the accounts that are required to record transactions 1-6.

Entries in **bold** are the balances in the T accounts before we record transactions 1-6. These amounts are taken from the statement of financial position in Exhibit 1. They summarise all the transactions that have taken place before that statement of financial position was prepared.

Trial Balance (after recording transactions 1-6)

Danish Pastry Ltd **Trial Balance 31 December 20x6**	**Debit** **€**	**Credit** **€**
Property, plant and equipment	11,000	
Inventory	4,000	
Receivables	5,000	
Prepayments	250	
Bank	5,800	
Equity share capital		10,000
Retained Income (op. 9,700)*		9,700
Payables		3,200
Accruals		500
Revenue		101,300
Cost of sales (including purchases)	75,700	
Wages	3,300	
Light & heat	1,400	
Insurance	250	
All other expenses	18,000	
	124,700	124,700

* Note: The opening balance on the retained income account is used in the trial balance rather than the closing balance. This is because this trial balance is prepared before the transfer of the profit for the year to the retained income account. When the financial statements have been prepared from this trial balance all of the income statement accounts (revenue etc.) will be transferred to the retained income account. This will increase retained income by 2,650 and reduce all the income statement accounts to zero in preparation for next year's transactions.

Chapter 7

Exercise 7.1 Solution

A Ltd. buys a machine for €50,000. The machine is expected to last 8 years and be worth €10,000 at that time.

(a) Calculate the depreciable amount.

Calculation of Depreciable Amount

	€
Cost of machine	50,000
Less residual value	(10,000)
Depreciable amount	40,000

(b) Calculate the annual depreciation charge on the machine.

Calculation of One Year's Depreciation Charge (using the straight-line method)

Depreciable amount	€40,000
÷ useful life	8 years
Depreciation charge for one year	€5,000

(c) Calculate the Net Book Value of the asset after 2 years.

Statement of financial position as at end of	**Year 2**	**Year 1**
	€	€
Non-Current Assets		
Machine at cost	50,000	50,000
Less accumulated depreciation	(10,000)	(5,000)
Net book value of Machine	40,000	45,000

=> The NBV of the machine at the end of year 2 is €40,000.

Exercise 7.2 Solution

(a) Calculate the depreciation for Machine A & B. Record this depreciation in the financial statements using the template supplied.

The Statement of financial position and Income Statement of Acid Ltd. With depreciation

Statement of financial position as at 31 December	**31.12.X6**	**31.12.X5**	**31.12.X4**
	€	€	€
Non-Current Assets			
Machine A at cost	12,000	12,000	12,000
Accumulated depreciation on machine A	(6,000)	(4,000)	(2,000)
Net Book Value (NBV) of machine A	6,000	8,000	10,000
Machine B at cost	8,000	8,000	
Accumulated depreciation on machine B	(2,000)	(1,000)	
Net Book Value (NBV) of machine B	6,000	7,000	
Total non-current assets	12,000	15,000	10,000
Current Assets			
Bank	26,400	12,900	5,000
Other asset and liabilities	11,100	7,100	10,500
	49,500	35,000	25,500
Equity			
Equity share capital	20,000	20,000	20,000
Retained Income *	29,500	15,000	5,500
	49,500	35,000	25,500

Income Statement for the year ended 31 December	**31.12.X6**	**31.12.X5**	**31.12.X4**
	€	€	€
Sales	120,000	110,000	100,000
Less cost of sales	(85,000)	(80,00)	(75,000)
Gross profit	35,000	30,000	25,000
Less expenses			
Depreciation on machine A	(2,000)	(2,000)	(2,000)
Depreciation on machine B	(1,000)	(1,000)	
All expenses (excluding depreciation)	(17,500)	(17,500)	(17,500)
Net profit	14,500	9,500	5,500

* Note retained income is equal to opening retained income (i.e. from the last statement of financial position) plus profit of this year. Retained income for X5 = Op. Retained Income (€5,500) + Profit for X5 (€9,500) = €15,000.

(b) Show the journal entries for depreciation in each of the three years

20x4

Machine A

Date	Account	Debit	Credit
31.12.X4	Depreciation expense (IS)	2,000	
31.12.X4	Accumulated depreciation (BS)		2,000

Being Depreciation on Machine A for 19x4

20x5

Machine A

Date	Account	Debit	Credit
31.12.X5	Depreciation expense (IS)	2,000	
31.12.X5	Accumulated depreciation (BS)		2,000

Being Depreciation on Machine A for 19x5

Machine B

Date	Account	Debit	Credit
31.12.X5	Depreciation expense (IS)	1,000	
31.12.X5	Accumulated depreciation (BS)		1,000

Being Depreciation on Machine B for 19x5

20x6

Machine A

Date	Account	Debit	Credit
31.12.X6	Depreciation expense (IS)	2,000	
31.12.X6	Accumulated depreciation (BS)		2,000

Being Depreciation on Machine A for 19x6

Machine B

Date	Account	Debit	Credit
31.12.X6	Depreciation expense (IS)	1,000	
31.12.X6	Accumulated depreciation (BS)		1,000

Being Depreciation on Machine B for 19x6

(c) Prepare the Cost of Machine A T account, Accumulated Depreciation on Machine A T account and the Depreciation on Machine A expense T account for 20x4.

Debit **Cost of Machine A (BS)** **Credit**

Date	*Account*	*Amount*	*Date*	*Account*	*Amount*
1.1.X4	Balance	12,000			

Debit **Accumulated Depreciation on Machine A (BS)** **Credit**

Date	*Account*	*Amount*	*Date*	*Account*	*Amount*
			31.12.X4	Depreciation expense	2,000

Debit **Depreciation Expense on Machine A (IS)** **Credit**

Date	*Account*	*Amount*	*Date*	*Account*	*Amount*
31.12.X4	Accumulated depreciation	2,000			

(d) On 31.12.X6 the company disposes of Machine A for €6,500 in cash. Record this transaction in the spreadsheet below.

Statement of financial position as at 31 December	**31.12.X6**	**Disposal**	**After Disposal**
	€	€	€
Non-Current Assets			
Machine A at cost	12,000	12,000 cr	0
Accumulated depreciation on machine A	(6,000)	6,000 dr	0
Net Book Value (NBV) of machine A	6,000		0
Machine B at cost	8,000		8,000
Accumulated depreciation on machine B	(2,000)		(2,000)
Net Book Value (NBV) of machine B	6,000		6,000
Total non-current assets	12,000		6,000
Current Assets			
Bank	26,400	6,500 dr	32,900
Other asset and liabilities	11,100		11,100
	49,500		50,000
Equity			
Equity share capital	20,000		20,000
Retained Income (op 15,000 +14,500)	29,500		30,000*
	49,500		50,000

Income Statement for the year ended 31 December	**31.12.X6**	**Disposal**	**After Disposal**
	€	€	€
Sales	120,000		120,000
Less cost of sales	(85,000)		(85,000)
Gross profit	35,000		35,000
Less expenses			
Depreciation on machine A	(2,000)		(2,000)
Depreciation on machine B	(1,000)		(1,000)
Profit on sale of machine		500 cr	500
All expenses (excluding depreciation)	(17,500)		(17,500)
Net profit	14,500		15,000

* Note closing retained income is now op. retained income (€15,000) + profit for the year (€15,000) = 30,000.

(e) Prepare the journal entries for the disposal of machine A

Date	Account	Debit	Credit
31.12.x6	Disposal account	12,000	
31.12.x6	Machine A cost		12,000

Being transfer of cost of machine A to disposal account

Date	Account	Debit	Credit
31.12.x6	Accumulated depreciation on machine A	6,000	
31.12.x6	Disposal account		6,000

Being transfer of accumulated depreciation on machine A to disposal a/c

Date	Account	Debit	Credit
31.12.x6	Bank	6,500	
31.12.x6	Disposal account		6,500

Being proceeds of the sale of machine A

(f) Prepare the disposal account for Machine A

Debit — **Cost of Machine A (SOFP)** — **Credit**

Date	*Account*	*Amount*	*Date*	*Account*	*Amount*
31.12.x6	Balance	12,000	31.12.x6	Disposal a/c	12,000

Debit — **Accumulated Depreciation on Machine A (SOFP)** — **Credit**

Date	*Account*	*Amount*	*Date*	*Account*	*Amount*
31.12.x6	Disposal a/c	6,000	31.12.x6	Balance	6,000

Debit — **Bank (SOFP)** — **Credit**

Date	*Account*	*Amount*	*Date*	*Account*	*Amount*
31.12.x6	Balance	26,400			
31.12.x6	Disposal of machine A	6,500	31.12.x6	Balance	32,900
		32,900			32,900
31.12.x6	Balance	32,900			

Debit — **Disposal of Machine A (SOFP)** — **Credit**

Date	*Account*	*Amount*	*Date*	*Account*	*Amount*
31.12.x6	Cost of machine A	12,000	31.12.x6	Accum. Dep. on machine A	6,000
			31.12.x6	Bank	6,500
31.12.x6	Balance	500			
		12,500			12,500
			31.12.x6	Balance	500

Exercise 7.3

Dodgy Ltd. has a receivables balance of €1,000,000. It becomes aware that one of its customers is having financial difficulties. This customer owes €20,000 and none of this amount is likely to be recovered.

(a) Prepare a journal entry to write off the bad debt

Date	Account	Debit	Credit
…	Impairment of receivables (IS)	20,000	
…	Receivables (SOFP)		20,000
Being impairment of receivables			

(b) Prepare a journal to record the increase in the allowance for credit losses

Calculation of Increase in the Allowance for Credit Losses

	€
Allowance for credit losses	49,000
Old allowance for credit losses	0
Increase in allowance	49,000

Date	Account	Debit	Credit
…	Increase in allowance for credit losses (IS)	49,000	
…	Allowance for credit losses		49,000
Being			

(c) What figure will appear for receivables in Dodgy's statement of financial position?

Calculation of Receivables in Dodgy's Statement of financial position

	€
Receivables	1,000,000
Less impairment of specific bad debt	(20,000)
Less Allowance for credit losses	(49,000)
Increase in provision	931,000

(d) What figure will be expensed for bad debts in Dodgy's income statement?

Dodgy's Income Statement (extract)

	€
Expenses	
Impairment of receivables	20,000
Increase in allowance for credit losses	49,000

Exercise 7.4

1. €4,550, ANS = B

2.
Calculation of Expense for Impairment of Receivables

	€
Impairment of specific receivables expense (9,000+2,000)	11,000
Increase in allowance for credit losses (4,550 -1,000)	3,550
Total	14,550

ANS =E

3.
Calculation of Receivables in the Company's Statement of Financial Position

	€
Receivables	100,000
Less Impairment of specific receivable	(9,000)
Less Allowance for credit losses	(4,550)
Net receivables in the statement of financial position	86,450

ANS = D

4.
Calculation of gain or loss on disposal of Air Pump

	31 December
	€
Cost of Machine A	1,200
Accumulated depreciation (300 pa x 2yrs)	(600)
Net Book Value	600
Proceeds from sale	300
Loss on sale of asset	(300)

ANS = D

5
Calculation of Accumulated Depreciation for Machine

Depreciable amount (€60,000 – €10,000)	€50,000
÷ useful life	10 years
Depreciation charge for one year	€5,000
X 2 years depreciation	€10,000

ANS = C

6.
Calculation of Accumulated Depreciation for Machine

Depreciable amount (€40,000 – €10,000)	€30,000
÷ useful life	10 years
Depreciation charge for one year	€3,000
X 2 years depreciation	€6,000

ANS = B

7.
Calculation of Accumulated Depreciation for Machine

Depreciable amount (€59,000 – €1,250)	€57,750
÷ useful life	10 years
Depreciation charge for one year	€5,775
X 3 years depreciation	€17,325

ANS = D

Chapter 8

Exercise 8.1 Solution

(a)
- Equity – ordinary and preference shares
- Debt

(b)
Equity is the least risky from the firm's point of view. This is because it is not repayable and dividends do not have to be paid.

(c)

	€
Equity	
Equity share capital	10,000
Preference share capital	10,000
Retained income	50,000
Total equity	70,000
Non-current liabilities	
Loan	20,000
	90,000

Exercise 8.2 Solution

1. ANS = B

2. ANS = C

3. ANS = E

Exercise 8.3

	Kim	**Kate**	**Kevin**	**Keanu**	**Sum Across**
Assets					
Bank	+30,000	+45,000	+10,000	+10,000	95,000
Equity					
Equity share capital – Preference shares				+10,000	10,000
Equity share capital – Ordinary shares	+20,000	+30,000			50,000
Share premium	+10,000	+15,000			25,000
Total equity					
Non-current liabilities					
Long term debt			+10,000		10,000
					95,000

Exercise 8.4

1. ANS = B

2. ANS = C = €1,500,000 / €.75 = 2m shares

3.
Issued share capital increased by €750,000. This means they must have issued 1m shares at €0.75 each.

The total proceeds of the share issue were:
€750,000 in issued share capital
€250,000 in share premium
=€1,000,000 total proceeds / 1,000,000 shares issued = €1 per share ANS = A.

Chapter 9

Exercise 9.1 Solution

Statement of financial position of Know-it-all Consultants

	Transaction 1	2	3	4	5	6	7	8	9	10	11	Total
Non-current assets												
Motor vehicles				5,000 dr								5,000
Accumulated depreciation on motor vehicles									1,000 cr			-1,000
Office furniture			1,000 dr									1,000
Accumulated depreciation on office furniture									100 cr			-100
Total non-current assets												4,900
Current assets												
Receivables					26,000 dr		6,000 cr					20,000
Bank	30,000 dr	3,000 cr	1,000 cr	5,000 cr		2,000 cr	6,000 dr	2,000 cr				23,000
Prepayments												
Total current assets												43,000
Total assets												47,900

Statement of financial position of Know-it-all Consultants (cont.)

	Transaction 1	2	3	4	5	6	7	8	9	10	11	*Total*
Equity												
Equity share capital	30,000 cr											30,000
Retained income												14,400
Total equity												44,400
Current liabilities												
Accruals										500 cr	3,000 cr	3,500
Total current liabilities												3,500
Total equity and liabilities												47,900

Income Statement of Know-it-all Consultants

	Transaction											
	1	*2*	*3*	*4*	*5*	*6*	*7*	*8*	*9*	*10*	*11*	***Total***
Revenues					26,000 cr							26,000
Less costs												
Rent		3,000 dr									3,000 dr	-6,000
Wages						2,000 dr						-2,000
Office expenses								2,000 dr				-2,000
Depreciation on motor van									1,000 dr			-1,000
Depreciation on office furniture									100 dr			-100
ESB										500 dr		-500
Net profit												14,400

Statement of financial position of Know-it-all Consultants

	Total
Non-current assets	
Motor vehicles	5,000
Accumulated depreciation on motor vehicles	(1,000)
Office furniture	1,000
Accumulated depreciation on office furniture	(100)
Total non-current assets	4,900
Current assets	
Receivables	20,000
Bank	23,000
Prepayments	
Total current assets	43,000
Total assets	47,900
Equity	
Equity share capital	30,000
Retained income	14,400
Total equity	44,400
Current liabilities	
Accruals	3,500
Total current liabilities	3,500
Total equity and liabilities	47,900

Income Statement of Know-it-all Consultants

Revenues	26,000
Less costs	
Rent	(6,000)
Wages	(2,000)
Office expenses	(2,000)
Depreciation on motor van	(1,000)
Depreciation on office furniture	(100)
ESB	(500)
Net profit	14,400

Exercise 9.2 Solution

Leopold Broom Solution

Part (a) In this part we must prepare journal entries for Leopold's transactions and then record them in T accounts. Some of the T accounts have opening balances that are contained in the trial balance given in the question.

(A) Journal entries

		Debit	***Credit***
DEBIT	Bank	125,000	
DEBIT	Receivables	125,000	
CREDIT	Sales		250,000

Being recording of sales 50% cash sales 50% credit sales
Broom's bank increased by €125,000 and we create a receivable asset of €125,000. The other side of the transaction is a credit to Sales which will end up in the income statement.

DEBIT	Bank	100,000	
CREDIT	Receivables		100,000

Being recording of receipt of cash from customers of €100,000
This reduces the receivable asset by €100,000 (=> Credit)
Of course, this means we are left with debtors of €25,000 at the year end. This is as asset because we will be paid this amount in the future.

DEBIT	Purchases	125,000	
CREDIT	Payables		125,000

Being recording of purchases of €125,000. We owe money to the people we bought the goods off so we set up a liability (payables) to reflect this. The other side of the transaction is to the purchases account which will end up as part of the cost-of-sales calculation in the IS.
REMEMBER DO NOT USE THE INVENTORY ACCOUNT FOR PURCHASES OR SALES

DEBIT	Wages expense	4,000	
DEBIT	Light & heat	3,000	
DEBIT	Rent & rates	2,000	
DEBIT	Insurance	4,000	
DEBIT	Payables (for purchases)	100,000	
CREDIT	Bank		113,000

These expenses are paid directly out of the bank.
=> the bank has decreased by 113k => credit bank
The expenses should be debited to expense accounts
The payment for purchases is a payment to payables.
Remember all of our purchases are on credit.

L. Broom Solution Part (A)

Bank

Bal	11,000	Wages (4)	4,000
Sales (250k /2) (1)	125,000	Light & heat (4)	3,000
Receivables (1)	100,000	Rent & rates (4)	2,000
		Insurance (4)	4,000
		Payables for purchases (4)	100,000
		Bal	123,000
	236,000		236,000
Bal	123,000		

Premises

Bal	30,000		

Motor vehicle

Bal	12,000		

Inventory

Bal	11,000		
		Bal	11,000
	11,000		11,000
Bal	11,000		

Receivables

Bal	25,000	Bank (1)	100,000
Sales (1)	125,000		
		Bal	50,000
	150,000		150,000
Bal	50,000		

Payables

Bank (4)	100,000	Bal	9,000
Bal	34,000	Purchases (2)	125,000
	134,000		134,000
		Bal	34,000

Bank loan

		Bal	30,000

Share capital

		Bal	1,000

Retained profits

		Bal	40,000

Sales

Bal	250,000	Bank (1)	125,000
		Receivables (1)	125,000
	250,000		250,000
		Bal	250,000

Purchases

Payables (2)	125,000	Bal	125,000
Bal	125,000		

Wages

Bank (4)	4,000	Bal	4,000
Bal	4,000		

Light & heat

Bank (4)	3,000	Bal	3,000
	3,000		3,000
Bal	3,000		

Rent & rates

Bank (4)	2,000	Bal	2,000
Bal	2,000		

	Insurance		
Bank (4)	4,000	Bal	4,000
	4,000		4,000
Bal	4,000		

Note for some of these accounts the balances refer to balances carried forward from the starting trial balance.

Broom International Traders Ltd.
Trial Balance as at 31 December 20X2

	Debit	*Credit*	
Bank	123,000		BS
Premises	30,000		BS
Motor vehicle	12,000		BS
Accumulated depreciation on			
Premises		3,000	BS
Motor vehicle		6,000	BS
Inventory at 1.1.X2	11,000		IS
Receivables	50,000		BS
Payables		34,000	BS
Bank loan (to be paid in full in 5 years time)		30,000	BS
Share Capital (1,000 ord. shares of €1 each)		1,000	BS
Sales		250,000	IS
Purchases	125,000		IS
Wages	4,000		IS
Light & heat	3,000		IS
Rent and Rates	2,000		IS
Insurance	4,000		IS
Retained profits		40,000	BS
	364,000	364,000	

Notes on this trial balance

This trial balance is the situation after all the basic transaction have been recorded (no. 1-3 in the question) but before the year-end adjustments for depreciation, bad debts, accruals and prepayments have been recorded.

Recording of the Year-End Adjustments

DEBIT	Depreciation expense	3,000	
CREDIT	Accumulated depreciation Premises		3,000

Being depreciation on premises (30,000 / 10 years)
We increase the accumulated depreciation by €3,000 and record an expense in the IS of €3,000. The accumulated depreciation account always has a credit balance. When it is subtracted from the asset cost account in the statement of financial position (Debit balance) it yields the Net Book Value (NBV).

DEBIT	Depreciation expense	3,000	
CREDIT	Accumulated depreciation motor v.		3,000

Being depreciation on motor vehicle (12,000 / 4 years)
See previous note

DEBIT	Bad debt expense (IS)	1,000	
CREDIT	Receivables		1,000

Being write off of specific bad debt. We want to reduce the receivables by €1,000 (we are owed €1,000 less) => credit receivables and record an expense of €1,000.

DEBIT	Increase in bad debt provision (IS)	2,450	
CREDIT	Bad debt provision		2,450

We want to set up a bad debt provision of 5% of receivables (€49,000).
This provision is in case any of the receivables turn out to be bad.
We set up a 'liability' of €2,450 (this will be subtracted from receivables in the statement of financial position). In order to do this we must record an expense in the IS (debit increase in bad debt provision)

DEBIT	Light & heat (ESB) expense	1,000	
CREDI T	ESB accrual		1,000

We have used up light and heat for Nov and Dec X2 but we will not pay this bill until after the year end. Therefore we must increase the expense in the IS and also set up a liability for the bill we owe.

DEBIT	Insurance prepayment	1,000	
CREDI T	Insurance expense		1,000

We have paid the insurance bill for the year to 31.3.X3. We have only used-up 3/4 of this amount. At the year end we have a prepayment (asset) of €1,000 (4,000 x 3/12). This will reduce the insurance expense in the IS and appear as a current asset in the statement of financial position.

L. Broom Solution Part (A)

Bank (BS)			
Bal	11,000	Wages (4)	4,000
Sales (250k /2) (1)	125,000	Light & heat (4)	3,000
Receivables (1)	100,000	Rent & rates (4)	2,000
		Insurance (4)	4,000
		Payables for purchases (4)	100,000
		Bal	123,000
	236,000		236,000
Bal	123,000		

Premises (BS)			
Bal	30,000		

Motor vehicle (BS)			
Bal	12,000		

Accum. Depreciation on premises (BS)			
		Bal	3,000
Bal	6,000	Depreciation expense (3)	3,000
	6,000		6,000
		Bal	6,000

Accum. Depreciation on Motor vehicle (BS)			
		Bal	6,000
Bal	9,000	Depreciation expense (3)	3,000
	9,000		9,000
		Bal	9,000

Depreciation expense (IS)

Accum. depr. premises (3)	3,000	Bal	6,000
Accum. depr. motor vehicle (3)	3,000		
	6,000		6,000
Bal	6,000		

Inventory**

Bal	11,000		
		Bal	11,000
	11,000		11,000
Bal	11,000		

Receivables (BS)

Bal	25,000	Bank (1)	100,000
Sales (1)	125,000	Bad debts expense (6)	1,000
		Bal	49,000
	150,000		150,000
Bal	49,000		

Payables (BS)

Bank (4)	100,000	Bal	9,000
Bal	34,000	Purchases (2)	125,000
	134,000		134,000
		Bal	34,000

Bank loan (BS)

		Bal	30,000

Share capital (BS)

		Bal	1,000

Retained income (BS)

		Bal	40,000

Sales (IS)

		Bank (1)	125,000
Bal	250,000	Receivables (1)	125,000
	250,000		250,000
		Bal	250,000

Purchases (IS)

Payables (2)	125,000	Bal	125,000
Bal	250,000		

Wages (IS)

Bank (4)	4,000	Bal	4,000
Bal	4,000		

Light & heat (IS)

Bank (4)	3,000		
ESB accrual (7)	1,000	Bal	4,000
	4,000		4,000
Bal	4,000		

ESB Accrual (BS)

Bal	1,000	Light & heat (7)	1,000
	1,000		1,000
		Bal	1,000

Rent & rates (IS)

Bank (4)	2,000	Bal	2,000
Bal	2,000		

Insurance (IS)

Bank (4)	4,000	Insurance prepaid (7)	1,000
		Bal	3,000
	4,000		4,000
Bal	3,000		

Insurance Prepaid (BS)

Insurance (7)	1,000	Bal	1,000
	1,000		1,000
Bal	1,000		

Provision for bad debts (BS)

Bal	2,450	Increase in bad debts provision (Receivables bal x 5%) (5)	2,450
	2,450		2,450
		Bal	2,450

Bad debts expense (IS)

Receivables (6)	1,000	Bal	1,000
Bal	1,000		

Increase in bad debts provision (IS)

Provision for bad debts	2,450	Bal	2,450
Bal	2,450		

Broom International Traders Ltd.
Trial Balance as at 31 December 20X2

	Debit	*Credit*	
Bank	123,000		BS
Premises	30,000		BS
Motor vehicle	12,000		BS
Accumulated depreciation on			
Premises		6,000	BS
Motor vehicle		9,000	BS
Depreciation expense	6,000		IS
Inventory** at 1.1.X2	11,000		
Receivables	49,000		BS
Payables		34,000	BS
Bank loan (to be paid in full in 5 years time)		30,000	BS
Share Capital (1,000 ord. shares of €1 each)		1,000	BS
Sales		250,000	IS
Purchases	125,000		IS
Wages	4,000		IS
Light & heat	4,000		IS
ESB Accrual		1,000	BS
Rent and Rates	2,000		IS
Insurance	3,000		IS
Insurance prepaid	1,000		BS
Provision for bad debts		2,450	BS
Bad debts expense	1,000		IS
Increase in bad debts provision	2,450		IS
Retained profits		40,000	BS
	373,450	373,450	

Notes:
This trial balance has been prepared after all of the year-end adjustments** have been recorded. In this trial balance the accumulated depreciation on the non-current assets has been updated for this year's depreciation expense and all accruals and prepayments are shown. The financial statements can be easily prepared from this trial balance.
** Inventory. Inventory is still shown at the opening amount in this trial balance. The updating of the inventory balance is usually the last adjustment that is processed and is done is conjunction with resetting all of the income statement accounts to zero in preparation for recording the next year's transactions.

Broom International Traders Ltd.
Income Statement for the year ended 31 December 20X2

	€	€
Revenue (Sales)		250,000
Less cost of sales		
Opening stock	11,000	
Purchases	125,000	
	136,000	
Less closing stock	(2,000)	134,000
Gross profit		116,000
Less expenses		
Inc. in bad debt provision	2,450	
49,000 x 5% = 2,450		
Light & Heat (3,000 + 1,000)	4,000	
Insurance (4,000 - 1 Qtr 1,000)	3,000	
Depreciation (Prem 3 + MV 3)	6,000	
Wages	4,000	
Rent and rates	2,000	
Bad debts	1,000	(22,450)
Net profit		93,550

Broom International Traders Ltd. Statement of financial position as at 31.12.20X2

ASSETS	€	€	€
		Accum.	
Non-current assets	***Cost***	***Dep.***	***NBV***
Premises	30,000	(6,000)	24,000
Motor vehicle	12,000	(9,000)	3,000
Total non-current assets	42,000	(15,000)	27,000
Current assets			
Inventory			2,000
Receivables		49,000	
Less provision		(2,450)	46,550
Prepayments (Insurance)			1,000
Bank			123,000
Total current assets			172,550
Total assets			199,550
EQUITY			
Capital 1,000 Ordinary shares of €1 each			1,000
Retained income (40,000+93,550)			133,550
Total equity			134,550
LIABILITIES			
Non-current liabilities			
Bank loan			30,000
Current liabilities			
Creditors		34,000	
Accruals (ESB)		1,000	35,000
Total liabilities			65,000
Total equity and liabilities			199,550

PART D.
Record the closing entries in the T accounts of Leopold Bloom.

DEBIT	IS (special IS 'T' a/c)	11,000	
CREDIT	Stock		11,000

Being clearing out of opening stock balance out of stock account at year-end.

DEBIT	Stock	2,000	
CREDIT	IS (special IS 'T' a/c)		2,000

Being recording of closing stock

DEBIT	IS (special IS 'T' a/c)	4,000	
CREDIT	Light and heat		4,000

Being clearing out of light and heat 'T' account to special IS 'T' account. The balance of €1,000 left on the light and heat 'T' account is the accrual and a statement of financial position item.

All the other IS 'T' accounts (or accounts where there is a combined IS and Statement of financial position 'T' account) should be cleared out to the special
IS 'T' account. At the start of next year (1.1.X3) we should only have balances on the statement of financial position item 'T' accounts. All the profit and loss
T' accounts should be reset to 0.

L. Broom Solution Part (D)

Bank

Bal	11,000	Wages (4)	4,000
Sales (250k /2) (1)	125,000	Light & heat (4)	3,000
Debtors (1)	100,000	Rent & rates (4)	2,000
		Insurance (4)	4,000
		Creditors for purchases (4)	100,000
		Bal	123,000
	236,000		236,000
Bal	123,000		

Premises

Bal	30,000		

Motor vehicle

Bal	12,000		

Accum. Depreciation on premises

		Bal	3,000
Bal	6,000	Depreciation expense (3)	3,000
	6,000		6,000
		Bal	6,000

Accum. Depreciation on Motor vehicle

		Bal	6,000
Bal	9,000	Depreciation expense (3)	3,000
	9,000		9,000
		Bal	9,000

Depreciation expense

Accum. depr. premises (3)	3,000	**IS**	**6,000**
Accum. depr. motor vehicle (3)	3,000		

	6,000		6,000

Inventory

Bal	11,000	**IS**	**11,000**
IS	**2,000**	Bal	2,000
	13,000		13,000
Bal	2,000		

Receivables

Bal	25,000	Bank (1)	100,000
Sales (1)	125,000	Bad debts expense (6)	1,000
		Bal	49,000
	150,000		150,000
Bal	49,000		

Payables

Bank (4)	100,000	Bal	9,000
Bal	34,000	Purchases (2)	125,000
	134,000		134,000
		Bal	34,000

Bank loan

		Bal	30,000

Capital

		Bal	1,000

Retained profits

		Bal	40,000

Sales

IS	**250,000**	Bank (1)	125,000
		Receivables (1)	125,000
	250,000		250,000

	Purchases		
Payables (2)	125,000	IS	**125,000**

	Wages		
Bank (4)	4,000	IS	**4,000**

	Light & heat		
Bank (4)	3,000		
Bal ESB accrual (7)	**1,000**	IS	**4,000**
	4,000		4,000

	ESB Accrual (BS)		
Bal	1,000	Light & heat (7)	1,000
	1,000		1,000
		Bal	1,000

	Rent & rates (IS)		
Bank (4)	2,000	IS	**2,000**

	Insurance (IS)		
Bank (4)	4,000	Insurance prepaid (7)	1,000
		IS	**3,000**
	4,000		4,000

	Insurance Prepaid (BS)		
Insurance (7)	1,000	Bal	1,000
	1,000		1,000
Bal	1,000		

Provision for bad debts			
Bal	2,450	**IS (receivables bal x 5%) (5)**	**2,450**
	2,450		2,450
		Bal	2,450

Bad debts expense			
Receivables (6)	1,000	**IS**	**1,000**

Income statement (IS) account			
Inc. in bad debt provision (5)	**2,450**	**Closing inventory**	**2,000**
Light & Heat	**4,000**	**Sales**	**250,000**
Insurance	**3,000**		
Opening inventory	**11,000**		
Depreciation	**6,000**		
Purchases	**125,000**		
Wages	**4,000**		
Rent and rates	**2,000**		
Bad debts	**1,000**		
Bal	93,550		
	252,000		252,000
		Bal	93,550

Note : **Bold figures** are the year end adjustments i.e IS ledger accounts being cleared out to the special IS ledger account.

Broom International Traders Ltd.
Trial Balance as at 1 January 19x3

	Debit	*Credit*	
Bank	123,000		BS
Premises	30,000		BS
Motor vehicle	12,000		BS
Accumulated depreciation on			
Premises		6,000	BS
Motor vehicle		9,000	BS
Inventory at 1.1.X3	2,000		
Receivables	49,000		BS
Payables		34,000	BS
Bank loan (to be paid in full in 5 years time)		30,000	BS
Share Capital (1,000 ord. shares of €1 each)		1,000	BS
ESB Accrual		1,000	BS
Insurance prepaid	1,000		BS
Provision for bad debts		2,450	BS
Retained profits (40,000 + 93,550 IS)		133,550	BS
	217,000	217,000	

Note

This is the opening trial balance for 20x3 (the year following the year we did the accounting for).

All of the income statement accounts have been cleared out to the special IS T account. This account is then added to retained income.

Chapter 12

Exercise 12.1 Solution

Lotti plc
Income Statement for the year ended 31.3.x6

	€'000
Revenue	2,300
Cost of sales	(1,510)
Gross profit	790
Distribution costs	(542)
Administration expenses	(313)
Other operating expenses	
Other operating income	50
Operating profit	(15)
Finance costs	(12)
Finance revenue	100
Profit before tax	73
Income tax expense	(30)
Profit for the financial year	43

1. Operating profit has been arrived at after charging the following amounts:	**€'000**
Audit fee	5
Directors' fees	25
Directors' salaries (200+50)	250
Salaries and wages (180+124+100)	404
Depreciation (28+10+29)	67

WORKINGS

COGS

	€'000
Opening inventory	500
Purchases	1,000
Closing inventory	(100)
Factory wages	100
Depreciation plant	10
	1,510

Administration Expenses

	€'000
Audit Fee	5
Depreciation - Fixtures & Fittings	29
Wages & Salaries - Admin.	180
Directors' Fees	25
Managing Director's Salary	50
Light and Heat	18
Stationery	6
	313

Distribution Expenses

	€'000
Carriage Outwards (delivery expenses)	100
Sales Director's Salary	200
Warehouse Expenses	10
Depreciation – Vehicles	28
Wages & Salaries – Sales	124
Selling Expenses	80
	542

Other Operating Income

	€'000
Rent Received	50

Finance revenue

	€'000
Dividends Received	100

Exercise 12.2 Solution

Mame plc
Income Statement for the year ended 31.12.x6

	Working	Note	€
Revenue			14,560,000
Cost of sales	1		(13,135,000)
Gross profit			1,425,000
Distribution costs	2		(234,375)
Administration expenses	4		(467,100)
Other operating expenses			
Other operating income			
Operating profit			723,525
Finance costs			(18,000)
Finance revenue			
Profit before tax			705,525
Income tax expense			(190,500)
Profit for the financial year			515,025

1. Operating profit has been arrived at after charging the following amounts:

	€
Directors' remuneration	
Fees	20,000
Other emoluments including pension contributions	210,000
Depreciation (11,000+22,000+57625)	90,625
Staff costs (423+120+53)	596,000
Audit fee	3,200

Statement of financial position of Mame plc as at 31st December 20x6

	Note	€
ASSETS		
Non-current assets		
Property, plant and equipment	2	1,978,375
		1,978,375
Current assets		
Inventories		1,210,000
Receivables (782,000-3,000-38,950)		740,050
Cash and cash equivalents		111,000
Total current assets		2,061,050
Total assets		4,039,425
EQUITY		
Equity share capital		500,000
Share premium		Nil
Retained income (2,437,900+515,025-230,000 div)		2,722,925
Total equity		3,222,925
LIABILITIES		
Non-current liabilities		
Interest-bearing loans and borrowings		150,000
Current liabilities		
Payables		467,000
Tax		190,500
Accruals		9,000
Total current liabilities		666,500
Total liabilities		816,500
Total equity and liabilities		4,039,425

Notes to the statement of financial position
Note 2 Property, plant and equipment

	Land	**Buildings**	**Vehicles**	**Total**
	€	**€**	**€**	**€**
Cost		(330+660)		
At 1/1/20x6	1,200,000	990,000	230,500	2,420,500
Additions				Nil
Disposals				Nil
At 31/12/20x6	1,200,000	990,000	230,500	2,420,500
Aggregate / Accumulated Depreciation		(242+55)		
At 1/1/20x6		297,000	54,500	351,500
Charged		33,000	57,625	90,625
Disposals				Nil
At 31/12/20x6	Nil	330,000	112,125	442,125
NBV 31/12/20x6	1,200,000	660,000	118,375	1,978,375
NBV 1/1/20x6	1,200,000	693,000	176,000	2,069,000

Workings

W1 Cost of sales	€
Opening inventory	1,300,000
Purchases	12,600,000
Closing inventory	(1,210,000)
	12,690,000
Dep. on factory (660,000/30)	22,000
Factory wages	423,000
	13,135,000

W2 Distribution costs	€
Selling expenses	59,000
Dep. of motor vehicles (230,500/4)	57,625
Packing costs	11,000
Impairment of receivables(3,000+11,800+38,950)	53,750
Sales salaries and wages	53,000
	234,375

W4 Administration expenses	€
Dep. on office buildings	11,000
Admin costs	102,000
Audit fee	3,200
Repairs and maint to office equip.	900
Directors' salaries	210,000
Admin salaries and wages	120,000
Directors' fees	20,000
	467,100

Chapter 13

Exercise 13.1 Solution

Statement of cash flows for the year ended 31.12.2005
Under IAS7

Operating activities	€'000
Profit before finance costs	619
Add Depreciation charges	50
Add loss on sale of plant	20
Change in receivables	(90)
Change in inventory	(260)
Change in payables	20
Change in accruals	10
Interest paid	(30)
Tax paid	(59)
Operating cash flow	280
Investing activities	
Capital expenditure (1,390+900)	(2,290)
Sales of non-current assets	20
Financing Activities	
Equity dividends paid	(60)
Increase in long term debt	320
Increase in equity	750
Increase/(Decrease) in cash	(980)

	Land	Buildings	P&M
NBV at start of year	500	400	160
Additions (?)	-	1,390	900
Disposals	-	-	(40)
Depreciation	-	(10)	(40)
NBV at end of year	500	1,780	980